SELLING YOUR PROFESSIONAL SERVICE FIRM

A PRIMER

DAVID C. BAKER

rockbench
PUBLISHING

978-1-60544-100-9—print

978-1-60544-101-6—Kindle

978-1-60544-102-3—Audible

Published by RockBench Publishing Corp, Nashville, TN

Printed in the United State of America

For speaking/consulting inquiries: www.punctuation.com

For bulk orders: www.rockbench.com

CONTENTS

INTRODUCTION

I've written this book because selling your business is quite possibly the biggest financial transaction of your entire life, and you've never done it before and will likely never do it again, and you really need to be smart about this.

I recently did a quick study on the likelihood that a firm in a particular, narrow vertical would have a successful exit—defined as someone else purchasing, for real money, a majority of your firm's equity.

It's not a great sales tactic to give you that number at the start of a book you just purchased, but the answer was roughly 1%, or 1 in 90. Ouch.

To use marketing firms as an example, roughly 1,000 firms are purchased every year in the U.S., of the roughly 90,000 firms that exist in the country at any given point. Of course, firms exist over an average lifetime that spans multiple years, so the odds of a successful purchase increase as a firm gets nearer its maturity, but they still aren't great.

While the odds of selling your firm are normally low, you can dramatically increase the odds with a few important changes.

But there's an important corollary to that truth, and it's this: There are many things you can do to improve your odds, turning that likelihood into a 1-in-4 chance that you'll sell your firm.

And then once you do set yourself up for a possible exit, there are some fantastic inside techniques to maximize the upside while also minimizing the risk.

This book is generally about selling your firm, but you can easily flip these principles around and be more successful at buying a firm, too.

We'll also cover many other elements of mergers and acquisitions (M&A) and the larger succession picture, including the requisite valuation of your firm.

This is not a textbook, though, and it doesn't cover some of the deeper intricacies of the legal and tax implications of a transaction. It's just a handbook to help you think differently about your options. You'll buy and sell more houses than you will businesses, and even though you'll need to hire professionals to help you, it's very much in your own best interest to understand the lingo and basic concepts so that no one takes advantage of you. So why not educate yourself?

The information in this manual comes from hard-earned experience in guiding 200+ transactions on both the buy- and sell-side, including searches, partnership splits, internal transfers, and everything else you can imagine.

Our experience comes from firms in the marketing, creative, and digital space, but the principles all apply to the larger professional services space.

Wherever you are on this adventure—just starting or wanting to do the next transaction without getting burned—enjoy the journey to one of the biggest decisions you'll ever make.

By the way, I wrote this book with no particular length in mind. The goal was to say what needed to be said, without any filler. To that end, you'll find some extended explanations where appropriate, and in other cases all you really need is a bulleted list to understand a concept. I'm assuming that you're smart—and that your time is valuable—which is why I've worked hard to keep this as succinct as possible.

One last note: The information in this book is designed roughly for firms in the $5–$50M range. Selling a smaller firm than this carries some unique challenges (which can be overcome), and firms bigger than this range have many more options. For example, the role of the principal and the nature of the earnout isn't nearly as important, there are more financing options, and there is generally less risk. So understand that the principles in this book apply most everywhere, but they are particularly apt for firms in that $5–$50M range.

1

PRETEND YOU CAN NEVER SELL YOUR FIRM

This is one of those rare instances in life when you can have your cake and eat it, too. All the things you do to make your firm more sellable are exactly the things that'll ensure that you don't feel the need to sell it.

But hidden in this chapter title is a critical truth, and it comes from playing the constraints game. In this case, the constraint is this: How will I run this firm if I never allow myself to sell it? Blair Enns, my podcast cohost, introduced this concept to me and I think about it all the time.

Asking yourself this question forces you to look long and hard at all the things that are unsustainable:

- Lack of profit.
- Long hours you're working.
- Elusive time off from the business, much less that crazy sabbatical you've dreamed of every night while falling asleep.
- Problem employees who don't fit the culture or lack the work ethic.

- Challenges around new business.
- Ungrateful clients who keep demanding more than they are paying for.
- Increasingly complex tax and legal and HR requirements, imposed on you by bureaucrats and politicians who've never worked an honest day in their lives.
- A client concentration challenge that leaves you as a supplicant, afraid to lose them.
- A pricing structure where you're trapped in a prison cell of your own making.

Now here's the remarkable overlap between your own version of the above list and an acquisition exercise: Fix those things and you won't feel as much pressure to sell because the business is working for you instead of the other way around.

Everything you do to make your firm more sellable will make you less likely to want or need to sell it.

But also, fix those things and a buyer is more likely to give you more money and on more favorable terms. (We're going to talk about how important it is to separate the price from the terms.)

Put differently: Fix those things and you have better options. You win either way!

2

WHY MORE FIRMS AREN'T SOLD

I'm talking specifically about professional service firms in the \$5–\$50M range. Firms above that are bought and sold regularly, but there are some things about this particular market segment that are true, and they create challenges in the M&A space. It's good to just acknowledge them, which is the first step in countering them in your specific situation.

Why are there virtually no outside investors in this space? You know, people who want to invest in a firm without actually running it? And what are the implications of that unique feature of our field?

Here's why I think our broad vertical of professional services is unique, and I'm specifically referring to consulting, marketing, engineering, architecture, legal, accounting, design, and so on.

- Principals are entrepreneurs and don't want a boss. If you've had an honest conversation with yourself, you know what a lousy employee you'd be. You're not afraid of hard work, but you don't like to be told what to do, you don't like restrictions and policies, and you want to change your mind and go in another direction quickly. You like making promises that are unhinged from reality and you absolutely love swooping in at the last minute and driving your team batshit crazy. All this means that the idea of an external investor who wants a say in how you do things won't likely fly.

- You don't make enough money to interest an investor. You aren't in it just for the money, for one thing, and so there are other things that flop your mop, as my mother used to say. You like the work, some of the clients, a few of your team members, and the glory of being a successful entrepreneur. Sure, the money is great, and it matters more as the years go by (and your kids go to college), but you didn't get into this field primarily to get rich.
- You love the work ... and your firm is small. The obvious connection between those two things is that you probably didn't grow up dreaming about running a 100-person firm and dealing with personnel, the bank, and enterprise resource planning (ERP) decisions every day. No, you wanted to be close to the work. The "people" part came later when the marketplace demanded that you grow, and you reluctantly pivoted a little bit away from *doing* the work toward building a *business* that did the work. But every stage of growth put more distance between you and the work; maybe you loved the change, maybe you didn't. The lack of management systems/processes meant that you were always a little "self-sizing" as the weaker kids (on the team) got flung off the merry-go-round, as it sped up, and only the strong kids could hang on.

- The barrier to entry is minimal. You'd typically only buy a business because it's a hassle to start one. Think nuclear facility or bank or utility, and not a lawn-mowing business or a stand at the farmer's market or a restaurant or a firm like yours. Today you could be an employee on the client-side, and tomorrow you could own a fully functioning firm, as long as you possessed any of the qualifications and certifications required by the field. If I want to own a creative firm, I'm probably just going to start it. If I want to own an accounting firm and I already have a CPA designation, why not? The lack of "regulatory capture" for this field is good for everybody, generally, but it also means that there is no protective moat around your firm.

You're really owner-operators. While the professional services industry—based on body count—is heavily skewed toward owner-operators, only 9% of the trucking industry (where I've borrowed the term from) is composed of owner-operators. Those who own and drive their own trucks make an average of $50K/year and drive an average of 101,000 miles/year. But they are in a field with tight regulation and heavy capital requirements, which is why it attracts investors who are essentially arbitraging the labor of others.

At first, the M&A market for professional service firms seems like a competitive mismatch. But you can play the game with intelligence and win.

We get the requisite education, where necessary, or we skip it. If you're a lawyer, you'll go to jail without the requisite background. If you're a consultant or a marketer, at the other end of that scale, it's all optional. But the common theme for everybody in professional services is that most people don't get into it primarily to make money, and so outside buyers look at those target firms and say, "Wow, it looks like nobody got into this to make money!" The most well-run firms, of course, pay a lot of attention to that, and thus their exits are spectacularly better, as you would expect.

Here's the bottom line: The "agency" you have (I'm using this term the way economists do) is a remarkable gift from the gods. Use it to run your firm exactly as you like, but unleash your creativity by making it a well-run enterprise that performs economically, does great work, and fosters an environment where the best people want to work alongside you.

There are virtually no external barriers to building a remarkable firm that you love being in charge of. And your exit will be more satisfying if you do it right.

3

ALWAYS BE OPEN TO SELLING

I know it feels like I've been playing with you so far. "You can never sell your firm!" "What the heck are you thinking—these things hardly ever sell, anyway!" And now, "But here's how to get ready to sell it."

The only reason I don't mind talking out of both sides of my mouth is that this is one of those rare scenarios where you win either way. Pretend you can never sell it and you'll be strongly motivated to fix the things about your business that annoy you. But really do plan to sell it because that forces you to run a firm that's built correctly.

Open But not Expectant

This chapter explains that last point, but with a specific twist: Always be open to selling, but don't try to sell it all the time, or you'll be disappointed if or when it doesn't. It's kind of like being prepared for a flat tire but then not thinking about it that much.

I wrote the last two books (*The Business of Expertise: How Entrepreneurial Experts Convert Insight to Impact + Wealth* and

Secret Tradecraft of Elite Advisors: Covert Techniques for a Remarkable Practice) from our cabin in the woods at the southern end of the Appalachian Trail, and I'm writing this book from a 2021 Newmar New Aire. I just need a separate place to write, and so I spend a lot of three-day weekends parked at different spots.

I travel with:

- A full set of tools.
- A 12v tire pump.
- A fiber optic inspection tool.
- Spare belts for the Cummins 8.9 diesel in the back, transfer fluid for the tankless diesel hot water heater, and everything needed for an oil/filter change on the Onan diesel generator.
- A spare lithium battery booster.
- A roadside assistance card from Coach.Net.

Oh, and the front steer tires have Retroband "run flat" inserts in case a front tire blows out. You kind of want to control a 39,000 lb. beast, especially since we're always towing a 4-door Jeep Rubicon. I'm not expecting to have a tire blow out, but I'll be prepared if I do.

You aren't expecting to sell your firm, either, but you'll be in a good place to do it if the stars align. And if you've purchased and are reading this book, you might have a real opportunity in front of you that requires you to proceed carefully, and you might wish you'd been more prepared when the opportunity popped up.

Real life does happen. Like a young client in Detroit who died of a heart attack, with no indication that it was coming, leaving the firm in the hands of his wife, who'd never spent a day in the business. Or the young client in NYC who was diagnosed with brain cancer and died six months later, leaving the firm to his No. 2, who had already been doing a good job running it, thankfully.

Those are dramatic examples of a real-life "change in control" clause, but your relationship with your business is far more likely to change slowly and almost imperceptibly. In the recent past, principals tired of dealing with clients before anything else, but these days, they seem to tire of dealing with the employees more. It just creeps up on you slowly, in very small doses, and you're left dreaming of a business that doesn't have employees or clients. What a fantastic business that would be, you smile to yourself!

More often than not, though, it's a very positive realization: "Hey, I'm at my prime. I've built something I'm really proud of. And I like building things more than running them. Besides, this career is just one of many I could be great at. I'd like to [carefully looks at notes about career choices that she wrote to herself right before going off to college, which still include several options that haven't been crossed off yet] try this next thing."

This is all pretty lofty sounding, but do you know what often causes the most introspection in your relationship with this business? It's about one year before your current lease expires, because that's the only long-term commitment you make to your business. "Do I want to do this another five years?"

It would be a bit too obvious to swap your LinkedIn profile image to indicate your openness to selling.

You may be at the edge of a specific transaction right now, which is why you're reading this. Or maybe not. Don't get too attached to this place. Keep an ear to the ground for great opportunities, because most of these will land in your lap organically and not because you're looking. It'll be accidental, unplanned, and serendipitous—not like having a flat tire at 64 mph, but rather like meeting someone at a party that you end up marrying.

You will have been taking good money out of the place every payroll, without fail, but you'll get to take some money off the table. Maybe it won't be eff-you money, as they say, but it could certainly move you farther from one end of the spectrum, where you're a greeter at Walmart, toward the other end, where it changes your family tree.

Run the business in a way that you don't get tired of it, but be open to the next chapter in your life.

4

DEFINING SUCCESS CORRECTLY

Speaking of having your cake and eating it, too: Running your firm well so that you don't need to sell it, but then having a better exit since you've been running your firm that way, will help you define success differently. I could have buried this concept in a medium-sized paragraph somewhere, but it deserves its own chapter so you can't miss it.

How you define success in running your business is so obvious that it doesn't need more than a few sentences to remind us what that means. It means three things, essentially:

- Paying yourself well, all the time, every payroll.
- Having a consistent, meaningful impact on grateful clients.
- Creating a culture you're proud of and where you don't dread going to work.

That's it. Nothing else needs to happen. If you do achieve a glorious financial exit, that's properly viewed as an added benefit and not a requirement. Some very entrepreneurial and resourceful and driven people start firms in order to sell them, but most of us aren't like that and shouldn't operate that way. Taken to an extreme, you'd leave all sorts of chaos in your wake as you chase the next deal in front of you. I admire people who can consistently achieve those exits, but that's a different world. You might run into someone like that who wants to *buy* your business, and that's fine, but remember that it's nothing more than a transaction to them and you'd better have your guard up so you don't get screwed by someone with a lot more experience than you have.

Success = Yes … or No

Think of normal success as running a business like I've described above, and that can be the foundation of a "[business] life well lived." So with that as a backdrop, how do you define success in a transaction?

Success should be defined as the right outcome rather than a specific one. More precisely: If this particular transaction is in my best interest, success is consummating the sale. But if this particular transaction is not in my best interest, success is not consummating the sale.

This is really, really important, because all the work and money you put into a possible transaction is what an economist would call a "sunk cost," and sometimes we don't want to abandon a sunk cost and so we keep pushing and pushing and pushing, and we end up screwing ourselves. But more important, the people negotiating on the other side will use that against you because you want it too badly.

You have to understand this process in a way that "no" can be just as correct as "yes" when you decide whether or not to proceed with a sale.

Always enter a potential transaction wanting the best outcome, and be sure that you hire advisors who want the same for you. And believe me, many advisors will be thinking of themselves and not you. Heck, if the transaction goes through, the commission they earn is even called a "success fee." But their success, getting paid, might not be success for you.

Success for you must be defined as doing what's in your best interest. If you *should* sell your business to this buyer, then success should be defined as maximizing the benefit and minimizing the risk to you. If you *should not* sell your business to this buyer, then success should be defined as finding that truth as early as possible to save you time and money so that you can avoid unnecessary distraction.

You have to be open to this and your advisors have to be open to this, and those are two separate things. You can't be afraid to ask all the hard questions, and your advisors can't be afraid to tell you the truth, by either urging you to slow down or dragging you across the finish line when you have last minute doubts before "Canon in D" by Pachelbel plays from piano and cello duo, like at your wedding ceremony.

Hire advisors who will work in your best interest and then define success as making sure that the right outcome happens as painlessly, as early, and as economically as possible.

5

THAT TRICKY 'TIMING' QUESTION

If you're interested in one day selling the firm you've created and built, how do you know when you've maximized your potential and thus the likelihood of success in finding a buyer? If you aren't ready to sell, how do you know what you should be working on?

The M&A process can feel like a black box. It's something most owners only go through once, so it's not worth an overinvestment of time on your part. However, having a basic understanding of what makes a firm "sellable" will make you a stronger decision maker and give you more confidence as you build toward an eventual exit.

But having said that, selling your firm rarely follows your plan. Instead, it's about being *sort of* ready, listening differently to the options that might surface, and then jumping on the fortuitous opportunity that often just comes out of nowhere.

There are still some timing issues that we can talk about, though, and so that's what this chapter is about: the tricky timing of a sale.

There are times when an opportunity to sell comes at you out of nowhere.

A Very Wide Range

If we're going to be honest, this process can begin unexpectedly and earnestly in just one day if you get hit by a bus. Fortunately, that's very rare. But if you don't want your life partner digging you out of the grave and killing you again in anger, make sure all the details are buttoned up. Document all the company passwords in a central place, have a No. 2 that you trust in place, make your wishes known while you're still somewhat lucid, and have a loose, existing relationship with an M&A advisor who can guide a successful transition that maximizes the asset you've built in the interest of the people you're leaving behind. That's the one-day scenario.

The next scenario takes 3–6 months: Winding your firm down in an orderly dissolution because you're just done, you haven't been able to find a buyer, or you got a less-than-ideal offer but you can't stay engaged even for a short earnout. This is also very rare, thankfully, but we'll talk about it in the next chapter just in case it applies.

The next longest period is the 4–11 months required to handle a transaction start to finish. It's unrealistic to assume that any great sale will require less than 4 months, but if it hasn't happened in a year or so, it's probably not going to happen—or shouldn't happen, if that much negotiation is required. Of course, the earnout, whatever that is, needs to be added to that timetable, although no one can force you to stay. If you're willing to leave some money on the table, you can always just say "adios" and walk out with a smile on your face and your laptop under your arm, fist-bumping the only people you've been honest with on your way to the parking lot.

The time from start to finish for a transaction can depend on what type it is, and what has forced it.

The longest transaction interval is probably selling the firm to an internal buyer, and this is especially true if you carry the note yourself. In other words, they aren't bringing outside money to the table, and so the sale is funded by the business you're selling. If you don't stay to shepherd that process forward, it might not remain healthy enough to actually complete the buyout.

Those are the four big categories and how time unfolds for each: from 1 day to 4 years.

Your Internal Clock

But aside from the actual transaction, how should you think about timing, especially when we're talking about your own internal clock? Think of "losing your engagement" as the penultimate step. It's the next-to-last step before the big, largely irreversible event that will almost certainly follow: You'll close your firm, you'll sell it, you'll take a sabbatical (often just to reaffirm what you already know), or maybe you'll fix whatever ails the firm so that your engagement rises again.

When you start to think about selling, you need to quickly address whatever is feeding your lack of engagement, or begin the process of moving to the next stage of your life.

The salient point I'd like to make is this: Once your engagement begins to dip, quickly "arrest the descent," as they say in flying, or you're going to hit the ground. Here are some reasons for that:

- Once your engagement wanes, it can quickly reach a tipping point after which there's no recovery.

- You don't want to enter negotiations where you can't bear the alternative: Saying "no" to the offer and pressing ahead with whatever energy you have left.
- Maximizing the total sale will often require sufficient engagement to get through the earnout period, if there is one, and some of these are up to 3 years long. So you have to anticipate how fast your engagement is dripping away before there's none left.

Other Timing Issues

There are other external timing issues besides your internal engagement level, too. I'll just mention them briefly:

- There are times when a bad year, especially if it's unusual in your recent history, might need to roll off the valuation, or at least get slotted into a year where the relative weight is lower, to put some distance between the present and the past and maximize your exit value. Say your EBITDA has been 24% in the most recent year, 2% in the year before, and 18% three years back. If the valuation uses a weighted average of $^3/_6$ for the most recent year, $^2/_6$ for the middle year, and $^1/_6$ for the first year, you really want that bad year to move from the middle slot to the earliest slot, as that'll reduce the impact of that single year by a full one-half. We'll talk more about that in a later chapter.
- The most recent financial results will always be the most relevant ones, but there are also times when you need to prove to a buyer that your most recent results aren't a strange aberration. Say your most recent EBITDA percentage is more than double

what you've historically achieved. The buyer is going to wonder if your most recent results are the new normal ... or some strange coincidence (almost always achieved on the back of a single client who became a client concentration challenge).

- The M&A market ebbs and flows just like the stock markets do, and you have to weigh your needs against where you are in your own particular story as it plays out. Maybe you do need to swim against the tide, but it'll take more effort and you may have to settle for a closer destination than you had originally imagined. Maybe you accept less, and move on to the next thing.
- Trends in a particular industry can spring up in a matter of months. Look at what the pandemic did to the travel and tourism industry, or how AI is disrupting dozens of industries, or how an incoming administration might impact regulatory capture.
- Finally, a client concentration issue (defined as one related source of revenue accounting for more than 10%–25% of your revenue, depending on which branch of the professional services you are in) can bring fast performance gains as well as unusual acquisition risks to the buyer.

But keep in mind that any timing issue that might be forcing your hand can also be used against you in the negotiations, so it's quite a dance to think about the when and not just the what.

And when it's all said and done, you may just need a little more time to find an alternative offer or two to bolster your negotiating position. A client came to us with an LOI that they were all ready to sign. They had just heard about us and asked us to take a look. We felt like it was a pretty bad offer, and we suggested that they should look around for something better. We found them two additional offers in our buyer pool. They didn't end up going with either, but used the leverage to more than double the offer they had in hand.

These things take time. If the buyer is desperate to close on the transaction, use that against them. If you're desperate to close, they'll probably use that against you.

6

TEN MAJOR OPTIONS

This primer focuses on the traditional sale, primarily, but there are many flavors of an M&A transaction. And by that I mean the many things that can affect a cap table. I'm going to list the most frequently utilized methods of transferring ownership and include just a few notes about each. If you are well past the point of considering all the options, just skip this chapter. It's long and you won't find it relevant.

But if you're just curious about your options and you find yourself in the early stages of pursuing something, we'll look briefly at 10 of these options, here, and include a few salient notes on each. Keep in mind that an entire book could be written on each of these. So while this chapter is very long (and thus skippable), it's really compressing 10 books into one chapter.

01: Merger

In an acquisition, you're essentially exchanging your company for money. It might be a stock sale or an asset sale, but it doesn't matter. You're selling something you own for money (cash at closing) and the promise of more money if things go well (the earnout). A merger—and we do a lot of them—is essentially a combination of many things to create a bigger pie.

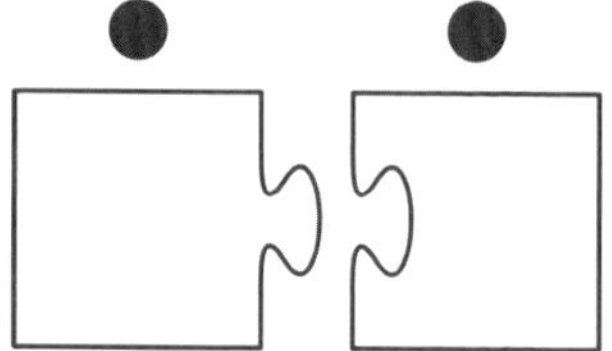

A merger combines two firms without one purchasing the other.

The "many things" include assets (cash, accounts receivable, equipment), obligations (client prepayments, what's owed on a credit card, etc.), client relationships, etc. Typically (but not always) a new corporation is formed into which both parties dump all their "many things," and then you may need an advisor to decide how to divide up that bigger, all-new pie.

What each party brings to the table will not always be equal, and that's where an advisor comes in. (Actually, you probably want to bring an advisor in very early in the process to see if it's even a good idea.) But then there are many decisions to be made, including:

- Who will own what percentage of the whole?
- If someone didn't bring that amount of matching capital into the new entity, how will that be accounted for?
- Who will do what on the leadership team?
- How will the new entity handle any personal guarantees that a former sole owner gave?
- How will leaders plan for the next step, when one of the new owners wants to leave?
- What happens to the parties' previous websites? Does it make sense to keep the more well-known company's name and fold the other one into it?

And a few dozen other big issues.

What usually motivates a merger instead of an acquisition?

- Neither party wants to work for anybody else. They still want to continue the entrepreneurial journey, even though that will now look different.
- They don't want to do it alone anymore. It's lonely, and no matter how valuable some of the senior members of the leadership team are, they still don't feel the same burdens of meeting payroll.
- Maybe one of the new partners is great at sales but not so much at the grind of getting things done profitably, while the other is really good at that but hates sales and always puts it off.
- Maybe the two firms have already worked together, side by side, for the same clients, and enjoyed it. And so this is a natural next step.
- Each firm might have a client concentration challenge, and now that same percentage is a much smaller part of the whole thing.
- It's a way for the older partner to find a successor, but in a more creative way.

This last motivation drives a fair number of mergers. The older partner has settled into running the firm, there aren't as many great exit opportunities as they'd like, no internal candidate has shown the willingness to "pay" for his shares, and so the hunt is on to find a younger partner to merge with. It's not announced, but the next step is to buy the older owner out slowly over time.

02: Partnership

This book isn't about partnership, but it would be really odd to not at least address the issue, however briefly. So here are the advantages of having multiple partners, as well as a few key suggestions on how to make that happen.

This option adds an external equity partner to an existing company structure.

Advantages of Multiple Partners

You can have too many partners, but for the purpose of this section, let's assume we're talking about an ownership group of two or three equal partners. What are the advantages?

- There's tremendous emotional benefit to being shoulder to shoulder with someone else at the plow, sharing the highs and lows of entrepreneurship, tough staffing calls, client disagreements, downturns, etc. This isn't reason enough to have a partner, but it's very powerful. If you want this sort of support without a partner, I'd recommend having an open-book relationship with a few peers or joining a community of fellow principals.
- A built-in succession plan is relatively easy to pull off, assuming that you aren't the same age or don't run out of engagement at the same time.

The key to pulling this off well (instead of self-destructing) is to fashion a strong, fair partnership agreement; if you do that, the firm is far more likely to gracefully navigate the departure of a partner.

- It's so much easier to focus on your own strengths if you have a partner. Anybody who hates new business but who has a partner who loves it knows exactly what I mean. But the key here is to not have a "stack of plates" partnership where you each run separate firms, but rather a slightly overlapping Venn diagram.
- You shouldn't have more than 6–8 direct reports, and multiple partners makes it easier to effectively manage a team, especially in a large firm.
- An obvious diversity of opinions is useful. Maybe it's male/female. Or maybe it's racial. Or maybe it's "hard charger" versus "empathetic listener." If you want that and don't want a partner, then work hard at being self-aware and valuing the opinions of other people on your team, especially.
- And finally, it's easier to get away or even take a sabbatical when there's someone to cover for you.

Some Specific Suggestions on Partnership

If you go this route, here are a few very specific suggestions:

- See the "stack of plates" analogy above. That's the most important. Roles should be different and take advantage of specific capabilities. Divide and conquer.
- Make sure that every initiative is headed by a specific partner and not the partners as a group.

- Have strong legal agreements, where nonparticipating spouses or common-law partners are a party to those agreements. A divorce that an individual partner faces is by far the most common legal jeopardy for a firm.
- Any partner who owns 20% or more should be paid equally, and no partner should be on a commission structure. Otherwise, it just highlights what one or more partners might view as unequal contribution.
- Absolute trust is essential. That trust erodes when a partner goes behind another partner's back and buys a shit domain for $100k after being overruled (that's a true story), there's an affair with a team member, stealing, etc. Rebuild that trust immediately through all the hard conversations that follow ... or move on.

Advantages of Being the Sole Owner

Having extolled the advantages of partnership, it's worth noting the other side. I wish I had stats for this, but it strikes me that most firms do not have multiple partners. What are those advantages of going it alone?

- Since I don't believe that there is any boost to economic performance for firms with multiple partners, we should necessarily conclude that there's actually a financial tax on having them. Turn that around and you can see that a single partner can be more highly compensated. In fact, in our "Principal Compensation Normalization" algorithms, we assume that a single principal will earn between $70K–$155K more if they don't have a partner. And that only accounts for the fixed comp and not what happens when you split profit distributions.

- Decisions are faster and often carry better calculated risks. With multiple partners, decision making is slower and less remarkable, because the rough edges get knocked off as the issues get masticated to death until they finally emerge with an announcement: "Look, we finally made a decision! And it's not remarkable!"
- Your key team members will feel like there's more opportunity to grow through advancement because there aren't partners clogging up all the high-level seats.
- Performance issues can be more readily fixed. To me, every partner is a stump in the swamp that needs to be navigated around because they can't be fired. (I'm still working on this empathy thing I keep hearing people talk about.)

If you are looking for a business partner, don't, because you'll almost always settle. Let it happen naturally.

Breaking Up a Partnership

And now, for a completely different slant on this, maybe the next step in your succession plan is removing a partner. Let me address that briefly in this same section.

The higher the partner count, the more likely it is that you'll remove one. When we begin advising a firm (about something other than partnership issues) and we hear that there are four or five partners, my first unsaid thought is "well, that won't last long." This is particularly true if the sum of the partners is greater than, say, 20% of the entire team count. So if you have four partners in a 20-person firm, that might stick. But I can guarantee you that four partners in a six-person firm ain't going to last long.

So that brings us to the process of removing a partner. That's not what this book is about, but I'll offer you a little insight into the scenario that's most likely to impact the cap table. For the sake of space, I'll just bullet-point these:

- The person who needs to be voted off the island is either a) not a cultural fit or b) you realized, after including them as a partner, that they are a great doer and not a leader, and thus can be replaced with someone who doesn't share in the profits or muck up the decision making.
- By the time you get around to doing something about this, you've realized it for more than a year, had private discussions to deal with it, and a few employees have questioned why they are a partner.
- It's going to be ugly. Face it. This will be a blow to that person's ego and there's no way around it.
- Separate ownership and compensation and you'll see your way through this. Owners get paid for what they own (via profit distributions and the sale of an equity stake), for what they do (via payroll), and for the unique, additional risk that they might take (via a shareholder loan, for example).
- Have a vote and dismiss the "doing" part of that equation. Include a severance package if it's appropriate, but stop their pay. Make sure you follow the bylaws precisely so that your actions cannot be successfully challenged.
- Stopping their pay will put pressure on the portion of what they "own." You won't want them as a shareholder, they won't want to own something over which they have little control, and the emotional

burden will eat away at all the parties until this is solved.

- The longer this drags on, the more pressure there will be to settle it, but you can offer incentives to settle it more quickly, like fixing any non-compete issues, giving them some clients, making it appear by mutual consent to the public, offering them a warrant should a majority of the firm sell to a third party within a certain specific period of time, etc.

Bad partnerships seldom get better. They need to be excised before the entire body rots from within, and you know whether this applies to you.

03: Internal Sale to Key Employee

This option comes up frequently, but because it seldom involves significant capital in exchange for whatever equity the joining partner brings to the table, it doesn't merit much treatment in a book about successful exits. But still, here's a framework for how to think about it, in two parts: Are you ready to offer partnership to a key employee, and then is that person ready to commit to making it happen?

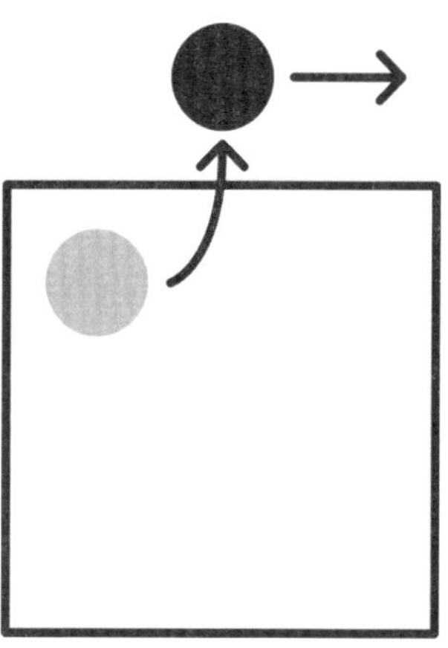

Moving an existing employee into a (majority) ownership position via a sale.

Are You Ready?

We put a lot of these together (and pull some of them apart), but here are a few things we'll ask a principal to see if they are ready:

1. Are you ready to make it public? There are no healthy partnerships that are also secret, but sometimes a principal wants to make someone a partner—to keep them at bay or whatever—but they don't want others to know about it quite yet. The typical reason is because it will signal that someone else has been excluded. See the next point.
2. If this is part of a succession play (in other words, you're leaving the firm soon), are you willing to designate one person as the primary lead partner? This, too, often comes from the same pressure: "There are three people who want to be minority partners, and none of them has enough money on their own, so I'll just arrange a marriage and increase the chances of this working if they can do it together." Wrong. Pick a lead partner, and let that person assemble their own team.
3. Are you willing to be transparent about everything, including your own pay? There should be no secrets. Eventually a principal will share financials, but often they'll want to limit disclosure of how much they make personally, which is silly. A junior partner will expect you to make more, and the more you make, the more alluring partnership is. You just have to get over it.
4. When you do announce this new partner, will most of the adults in the room nod their heads, agree that it's a good idea, and wonder why it didn't happen earlier? Moving someone to partner status should just confirm what's kind of already true. The team should accept it ... and even welcome it as an

excellent idea. This person that you are making a partner will have already paved their own way by impressing most of the right people.

5. Is there enough upside in this action that you are willing to accept the downside if it doesn't work out? Here I'm talking more about the initial discussions, when you broach partnership, but haven't concluded the process yet. When you ask someone to marry you, there's going to be a yes or a no—the status quo is no more. So don't initiate this beautiful process unless you're willing to let that person walk if it doesn't work out.
6. Are you willing to make decisions collaboratively? These decisions will be a tad slower, a tad safer, and a tad less remarkable, but the process will not be the same. You won't have a boss, per se, but you'll have less freedom to move forward. That isn't all bad, but it's different.
7. Do you have disparate roles? Your two roles shouldn't look like a stack of plates where comparison and overlap are inevitable, but rather intersecting rings where you lead a distinct area, trusting the other partner to do the same in a different area of strength. Have you worked all that out?

The early ones to test yourself on are 1 and 3, and then the rest will fall in place if it's a good idea. But then there's the question of whether that key employee is really ready for partnership.

Are They Ready?

Exploring a partnership is like seeing a truck rolling toward you. Throw obstacles under the tires, and if the truck keeps moving after rolling over all of them, it's maybe meant to be. I don't mean that to be negative, at all, though. I think a strong partnership is a wonderful thing.

But partnerships are not as wonderful as the would-be partner might think, and there needs to be some careful evaluation. At the beginning of the exploration, the would-be partner is looking mainly at the pros, throwing the cons behind their back as they move forward. So a legitimate partnership discussion needs to bring both the pros and the cons into view so that everyone can make an informed decision.

When a would-be partner hears the downsides of partnership, they might want to keep moving forward, which is fantastic, because then you have a fully informed participant who still wants to do it. But if, after hearing the downsides, they start second guessing themselves about what they thought they wanted, we have the opportunity—as advisors—to redirect our efforts to a less involved—but still motivating—arrangement that everyone will be happier with.

These are the harsh realities of being an equity partner, and it's important that every would-be partner understands the risks and challenges:

1. An equity shareholder will likely have a stronger, more enforceable non-compete than a key employee will. Under current law, a key employee can usually leave and start a competing firm across the hall, but owners have other fiduciary responsibilities that are more easily enforced.
2. An equity shareholder's nonparticipating spouse or common-law partner will need to be a party to an agreement. None of the existing partners will want an uninvolved shareholder with an antagonistic relationship with the firm, and so this eventuality

will need to be addressed. This is the most common "call" on the ownership agreement and/or bylaws, too. So when a partner's personal relationship goes bad, it will need to trigger two things: a price for those shares and the terms under which they will be purchased over time (e.g., equal payments over five years at a specific interest rate). You may think this won't apply, but you'd be wrong. Imagine a married employee who becomes a 30% partner. A year later they get a divorce, and that partner's former spouse now owns 15% of your firm, and they almost always have an adversarial relationship with the other partners and the firm itself. This will always be true unless the uninvolved spouse is a party to the partnership agreement or has signed a prenuptial agreement that addresses this. The reason this is on the list of "cons" is because some partners can't bring themselves to have this discussion and work out the agreement, and so if they are not willing to have that conversation with their spouse, they are not ready for partnership.

3. An equity shareholder's compensation will drop when the firm faces economic uncertainty, even when employee salaries are fully funded to retain their services during that difficult time.
4. An equity shareholder might receive a "capital call," requiring them to infuse an amount of capital that is proportional to their ownership position.
5. An equity shareholder's personal credit will be revealed (and could become an issue) when negotiating loan or lease agreements. A credit check will almost always be required at some point. Is the new partner comfortable with what that will reveal?

6. Where required by a financial institution, a personal guarantee from all equity shareholders will be required, making them "jointly and severally" liable. That means that the bank can go after all personal assets until the loan is satisfied. Everybody is on the hook for everything, and not just whatever portion of the partnership they own.
7. Bankruptcy can erase obligations, but two things are impervious to bankruptcy filings: student loans and taxes. When a company defaults on its taxes, or maybe a key employee doesn't remit withheld taxes, or in the worst case scenario doesn't pay them at all, the shareholders can be held responsible, even when they had no knowledge or involvement in the issue. Partners can indeed become responsible parties for any tax issues.
8. Usually, the new equity shareholder must purchase equity, and that money will come from personal savings, home equity, a loan from a commercial entity, or friends and family. Or failing an actual buy in, a reversal (when the company buys it back) can be conducted with the same discount. The point is that equity ownership usually requires funds, and that point alone can make a transaction difficult.

Some would-be partners are aware of all these things and are excited to continue. Others wonder if there's a simpler, less risky way of achieving the end goal, and that's where you should guide the discussions if it's appropriate.

04: Private Equity Investment

Like I noted at the outset of this chapter, an entire book could be written about how to manage an acquisition of your firm by a private equity (PE) investor. In some ways, everything you learn in this book will be relevant to that scenario, but here's what's unique about being purchased by a PE firm.

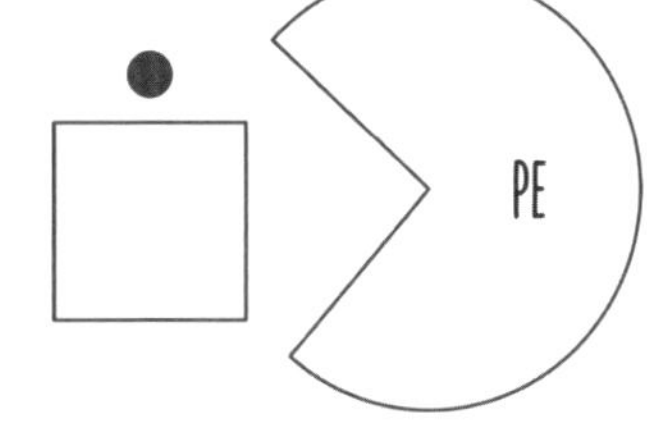

Allowing a private equity firm to purchase your firm, along with the expectation that it will grow quickly and be sold again.agai

- The purchase is always about money. It might not be money right now (your contribution to the profit), but it will always be about money later (a better return on a later sale because your firm is part of the mix).
- They will care a lot about growth. In fact, the earnout might be pegged to this. It might be a 5- or 10-year horizon, but they will always want a return "on" (not "of") capital to the original private investors, and they'll want a really significant return, too.
- You may not get much interference at the beginning, but the PE people will be breathing down your neck if your firm's performance isn't meeting expectations. They might even dismiss you if they deem your leadership insufficient to meet the moment.
- Assume that your firm will be part of a portfolio of related businesses. That may come with expectations that you'll play nicely with the other firms.
- Other people are going to assemble the partner firms purchased by this fund. This can be bad, for obvious reasons, but it can also be good. Maybe you install a great leadership team to continue guiding what you've built and you get the opportunity to

move to a "sister" firm that the PE firm purchased in order to turn things around there.
- There may be a lot of cross-selling between the various PE-purchased firms. This can be bad, because you'll be expected to sell their stuff to your clients, but it can be good, because you'll have new places to sell your stuff.
- The PE people will be professional negotiators who have a lot of leverage, little entrepreneurial experience (in your field, at least), and confidence that they are in the driver's seat. They view your firm as "nice to have" but they also believe that there are many options out there. They may view you as interchangeable.
- The relationship you have with your clients, and the general vibe about your firm in the marketplace, will change a bit. Your current and prospective clients might look carefully for signs that you're running the prices up and taking advantage of them, and they'll assume that the relationship they have with you may be more transactional than before. That might not be true, but that's the stigma you'll be fighting.

Note that what I've described above assumes that the PE firm is purchasing 100% of your equity. They may only purchase a portion, in a traditional sense, with an option for more. Or quite frequently you'll see that a portion of the sale is allocated to rollover equity, where a percentage of your stock isn't paid for in cash at closing or during an earnout, but is exchanged for a smaller percentage of the bigger whole. This is also referred to as a "second bite of the apple"—you hope that they grow the value of the whole and you'll be able to cash out of that later. You're essentially giving up control over that small percentage, leaving the outcome largely in their hands, but it can also be a good way to diversify your holdings. In other words, your own earnout might not meet your expectations, but your rollover equity might do very well. You'll be pressed to accept a portion of the sale as rollover equity, and it's often a good signal to the buyer if you do accept that, and it usually works out in your favor, too, if your horizon is long enough to wait for it.

From the PE firm's perspective, allocating some of the purchase into rollover equity does two things:

1. They need less cash now to consummate the deal.
2. They lock your interests and theirs together, since you have a vested interest in how the larger firm does, too.

05: Sale to a Current Client

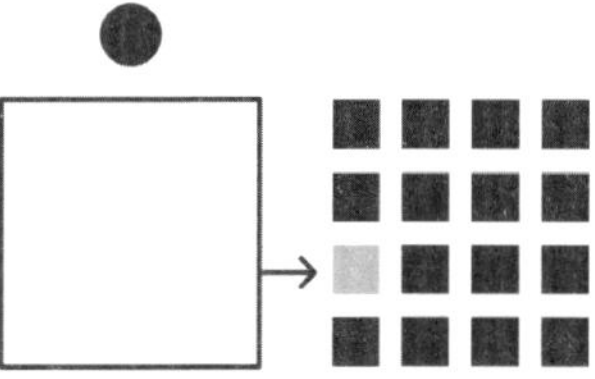

Selling your firm to a current client is rare, and always emerges from a longstanding relationship in which you each have become central to each other.

In our experience, only about 2% of transactions involve the sale of a firm like yours to one of its current clients. We have managed multiple transactions like this, and it can be a great option in certain cases. These sales are particularly unique because they always emerge from an existing client concentration challenge. In other words, the eventual buyer is already a client, but over time they have come to represent a larger and larger percentage of your revenue. You work hand in hand. There's deep trust. You're almost an in-house department of attorneys or developers or accountants or whatever.

It starts with a joke. A light comment in passing. Maybe

you're celebrating a recent win together, where there have been many late nights and you've pulled off this great success. You're celebrating at a bar. You've each had two drinks and you've let your guard down, and you blurt out: "Hey, that was fun. Maybe you all should just buy us so that we can keep doing these great things together!" You mean it in fun, but there's also a subconscious level of truth to it.

The next day, you think about what you said and you realize how both firms have grown together, and how you've also lost some of your leverage. You've been so busy working for this big client—staffing for them, being upstream before any implementation begins, knowing all their inner workings—that you've neglected your own business development. Heck, it's all you can do to keep up with what your client keeps wanting from you, and there's certainly no time to find other clients. And how would you serve them if you landed them?

Slowly, inexorably, you find yourself in this moment. This great client represents 55% of your billings. Maybe even 80%, or whatever. The thought of just joining forces has crossed both of your minds, and so the dance begins.

What's unique about this situation?

- There's only one buyer, so you don't have the normal leverage. Any outside buyer would view your relationship with this one big client with some skepticism. "What if they lose that client? How will that client feel about the ownership of their key partner changing hands?" This is especially true if any other buyer is a competitor to your big client.
- Smart clients don't really want to pay a lot of money to purchase their own revenue. In a traditional transaction, they are buying a revenue stream that's generated from other companies, but here, most of

the revenue is money they are sending to you in the first place.

- Almost all of your other clients are going to go away in the short term, and your ability to find other clients to replace them could be quite a challenge.

For all these reasons, a transaction like this is rare, but when the stars align, it's a really good thing. In fact, there's hardly ever an earnout, except maybe to ensure that you stay. In other words, the purchase price is essentially guaranteed.

Here, it's particularly important that you have an advisor who can work with *their* advisors to ensure that your relationship with the client doesn't incur more risk than is absolutely necessary. If the deal doesn't, in fact, happen, it may go back to where it was before, but it may end entirely, and someone else needs to be your agent and shoulder the blowback.

06: Acquihire

This term comes from the combination of 'acquisition' and 'hire' and the result is a word that always messes up your spellchecker. As you would expect, the transaction is somewhere between the two on a scale of impact on the seller and risk for the buyer.

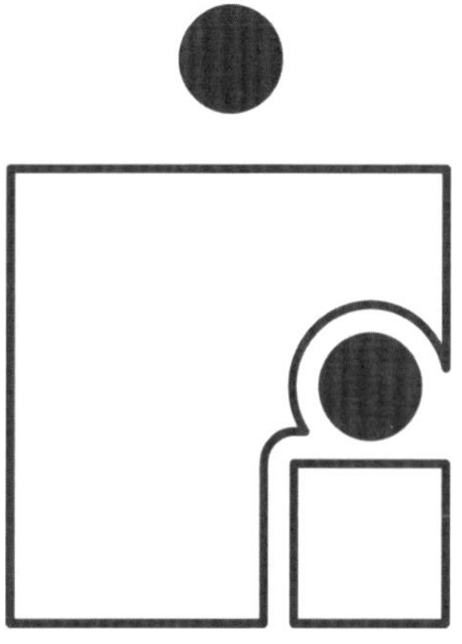

An acquihire refers to absorbing a firm in which the transaction is more than a merger (to the seller) but less than an acquisition (to the buyer).

An acquihire is always a fallback. An Option B, if you will. If a traditional acquisition is possible, that's always how it'll happen, but something is wrong on the seller's side and the value of that firm is impaired. Maybe there's little or no profit. Maybe the owner just doesn't feel cut out for entrepreneurship. Maybe new business has been a big struggle and the owner just hates every part of the sales process.

The seller might have even been a very strong firm, at one time, but something happened. It could have been a long, slow decay ... or the sudden loss of a large client. Whatever the circumstances, the value of the firm isn't what you might traditionally expect.

On the buyer side, there's a real reason for expansion, but maybe it's in the "nice to have" category and not a "must have" sort of thing. They might want to add a certain service offering or expand geographically or just add a whole bunch of employees at once rather than trying to hire them one by one.

If you think of an acquihire as a great alternative to just growing slowly by hiring people, here's where it might make sense for the buyer:

- It's faster. There's a leap in size.
- It's more newsworthy and can signal health to the marketplace.
- The people included in the "purchase" are largely proven and they know how to work together as a group. The culture is already there.
- They might be adding revenue and not just people. This depends, of course, because sometimes the lack of revenue is what throws this into an acquihire category in the first place.
- The transaction will come with clients which they may not have had access to before. They can cross-sell to them.
- They can add your clients' logos to the wall, overnight, building a stronger case for their experience.

And if you are the seller, not a lot of money might change hands, but you're still considering it because:

- Your team now has more rungs on the career ladder.
- You're tired of going it alone. In fact, you may even be largely done, and this is better than closing your firm.
- It opens up other opportunities for you down the road. If this makes it more likely that the firm that's buying yours can have an exit, perhaps you'll benefit from that.

How is this usually structured? There are typically four components of a transaction like this. Two are certain and two are optional:

1. You keep your balance sheet. It's not like someone is paying you for this. After all, you already own it, but your firm's working capital needs will disappear after the transaction, so you can take whatever book value there is and do something with it.
2. You get an employment agreement that is more guaranteed than your current payroll, which you might have deferred from time to time during the rougher periods.
3. You may get a signing bonus at the transaction boundary.
4. You may get some sort of override, where you are paid a certain percentage on the revenue from whichever clients come with you and stay for a period of time. Often this is a set percentage the first year, and then a reduced percentage the second year, and then all your clients are deemed to be "house accounts" after that.

One last note: You'll seldom hear an acquihire referred to by that name publicly. It's nearly always referred to as an acquisition, but all the insiders, and the people who can read between the lines, will know that it wasn't a traditional acquisition. But calling it that is a respectful way to announce what's happening.

07: Orderly Dissolution

You're just done. In fact, you're *so done* that you can't even fathom the notion of staying on during an earnout, especially when it means working for someone else. You're past the point of caring what the marketplace thinks, too, and this other venture you've been building on the side is really taking off, or you're at an age where not doing this anymore starts to get pretty appealing. So appealing that you think about it quite a bit.

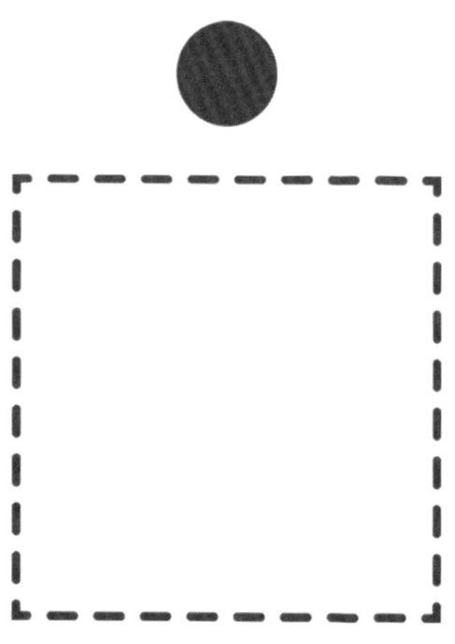

An orderly dissolution follows your own decision to close, rather than being forced to.

Maybe you've tinkered around with a transaction but it didn't appeal to you. Or maybe you pretended to care about new business but never quite got around to it, and the client that you've had for 17 years has signaled that things are going to change. Your current contact —the good friend that's been there from the start—is moving on, too, and you're getting a strong feeling that the new leader is going to switch things up.

There's no bankruptcy. You've run a tight ship and there's no appreciable debt. You're just done and that's it. But the one thing I'll suggest is that you at least find a firm where you can park some or all of your people, and do the same for your clients. That'll give both parties a place to land, and you may even make something from the client side if you make an arrangement to earn a commission on the work they retain.

08: Roll-Up

A roll-up is pretty much what it sounds like: One entity buys many (usually smaller) firms and combines them for a specific purpose. That specific purpose is usually a more advantageous sale to another entity, but the methodology allows for a much better exit than would otherwise be possible. Every so often you hear of such an entity exiting via a SPAC (special purpose acquisition company), but it's incredibly rare and we'll leave that for others to discuss.

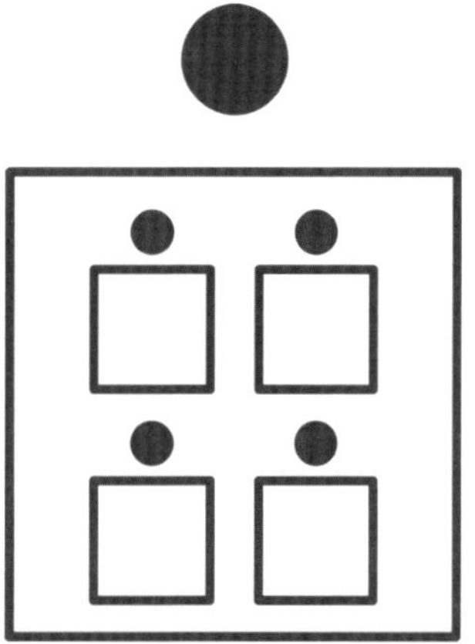

A roll-up is a process in which a third party assembles an eventual large entity by combining multiple firms, all for the purpose of a later exit of the whole.

These are the typical reasons why you might pursue a roll-up strategy on your own:

- Maybe something has changed in the marketplace, and potential clients are now wanting to buy certain services together, and so it makes sense to house those combined services under one roof. For example, maybe they no longer want to purchase fundraising and planned giving separately, and so a roll-up might combine the two on the way to also adding others, like a direct mail firm and a research firm and so on.

- Reducing a client concentration challenge is a frequent reason for a roll-up. Nothing might change in the service offering mix, but now, if two equal firms are combined, your 40% client concentration challenge sits at a more palatable 20%.
- You can often realize a more efficient use of resources by combining firms that all use those same services. For instance, one CFO can manage the entire combined entity, which might also apply to HR services and some of the other C-suite roles. You can also usually save on SaaS license fees, whether through bulk pricing or more leverage in negotiations.
- But the biggest reason to consider a roll-up is that it can take you across certain unwritten EBITDA boundaries. In some fields, you'll attract a higher multiple if your firm is above the $1M EBITDA boundary, and quite a bit more if it's above the $3M boundary and then maybe you hit another boundary at $10M EBITDA. So being a bigger firm, and thus a bigger target, is not just additive but exponential.

As you would expect, there are also some challenges to this. Here are some of the larger ones:

- How to get the smaller shareholders off the cap table. Buyers do not usually want to mess with all sorts of sellers, even if they don't have any effective voting rights because of their minority status. A firm that you might want to add could have offered minority positions to key employees in order to retain them, but that might not be practical in this new scenario. Yes, you probably still want to keep

them, but you might need to use a different method that allows you to achieve an easier later sale without their explicit permission.
- Dealing with the role that key leaders play can be challenging. You're not going to need two CFOs or COOs. Often this is solved because someone is ready to leave, anyway, or take a lesser role, but it can be messy.
- You might be creating some client conflicts. If one firm has Delta Airlines as a client and the other firm has American Airlines, you'll have to create what's called a conflict strategy to accommodate the concerns of either party.
- And finally, the culture is important. If you don't get this right, people will leave, clients will defect, and you'll be left holding an empty shell of something you thought had more value originally.

You might also be approached by an outside party that is attempting to build a roll-up, but keep in mind that they will studiously avoid that term because of the implications that come with it ("we're in it just for the money," "culture isn't as important," etc.). But you need to look for clues and force them to reveal that strategy. The most likely signal you'll see is what's called rollover equity, because that implies that you'll only get some of the proceeds from the sale now, when your firm's closing is scheduled, and the rest will occur later when the whole thing sells (if it does).

When you are approached as a roll-up candidate, you want to pay special attention to these factors:

- How your rollover equity will be diluted with each subsequent acquisition by the firm that's buying you.

- What happens to your balance sheet in the sale, because some seller candidates are approached because of their hefty book value, which is then used to fund later purchases, rather than their profitability.
- What control, if any, you'll have over the nature of those later purchases. This concern falls into two categories: the service offerings that will be bundled with yours and the culture of the added firm(s). On the first, your positioning might be dragged down because of the perceived expertise of that later addition; on the second, they might have a sales-driven culture vs. your expertise-driven one, etc.
- How to reverse the transaction should the roll-up not materialize.

09: ESOP

The intention behind ESOPs is noble, but the vehicle is flawed. That's the overview of this brief summary. The people who disagree with me on this are either ESOP advisors or recent ESOP graduates who haven't yet seen what'll happen to their ESOP down the road.

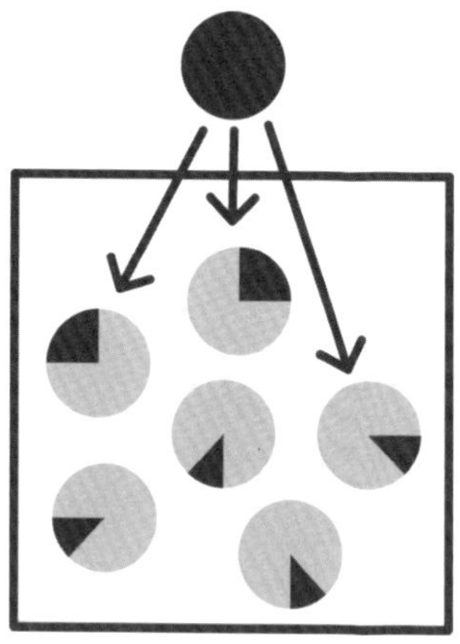

An ESOP is a tax-advantaged vehicle that allows the transferring of ownership to a legal entity that is then owned by the individual employees.

The ESOP (employee stock ownership plan) movement started with some lofty goals, but underneath it all is a massive tax advantage for the seller (this is only true for the U.S., U.K., and Ireland variants, which is why they are pushed so hard in the

U.S., especially). And the unbalanced narrative is fueled by the stakeholders in the movement itself. While an ESOP can (but seldom does) make sense in a large production or logistics or industrial environment, it very rarely makes sense for a professional service firm like yours, and that's why we'll not help you do one. Here's the "why" behind our stance.

Background

The ESOP movement is present in every developed country and its theoretical premise is really alluring: "If the team actually owns the company, their work will be different because they are working for themselves. They'll think like owners."

This makes perfect sense to me on its face, but there are two things missing from the equation:

- The role of entrepreneurial decision making, which often balances the short-term and the long-term. Employees (just like voters) tend to focus more on the now, without making the short-term sacrifices that will serve the firm's (or country's) longer-term success. Thus the trouble our Social Security system is facing in the USA.
- The structure of how an ESOP firm works—while the premise itself is good—violates many other important principles, and in the end it doesn't deliver as promised.

So where do the heavenly glories of ESOPs come from? One, from trade associations, which are continually publishing stats about how much more engaged the workforce is and how the profits keep rolling. And two, from eager advocates who are in the early years of an ESOPs life, before the negatives start to surface. Please look to independent sources before you believe all that.

Eight Problems with ESOPs

Rather than turn this section into a short book, let me just summarize the problems with an ESOP. In some cases, even one of these reasons should talk you out of it. But there are actually eight.

- **Safe, Unremarkable Decision Making.** First, please note that everyday workers have a voice, but no real vote. All the actual decisions are made by a committee of "administrator" types who try to please everyone and not fail. These folks are chosen primarily because of their tenure, but they are not entrepreneurs. ESOPs do not attract entrepreneurs but in fact spit them out. None of this will matter in the early days after the transaction, but it'll eventually catch up to them. Predictability takes the place of innovation.
- **Risk Concentration.** Say your kid finds a job that she's really excited about. It's a publicly traded firm, and she has the option of investing all her 401(k) in company stock. That's how much she believes in the firm's future. What would your advice be? A smart advisor would say to not tie your job to your retirement, because if it fails or even falters, you'll lose on both fronts. But that's what an ESOP does: concentrate an employee's risk. Yes, an ESOP can also have a 401(k), but if it does (most don't), it's not seriously funded. What makes this a little bit worse is a common theme in job offers from ESOP-owned companies: "Yes, your base salary is a little bit lower

than you'd otherwise get, but the bonuses are more substantial and within your control." Think of the backlash, about a decade ago, to the idea of a trustee or some other designated person making investment decisions over your own retirement account. Now, instead, every sensible firm allows "participant directed" retirement decisions. So I, as the principal, decide how we'll fund the 401(k), but you decide how you want to invest that money that's allocated to you. This does not happen in an ESOP. Your job and your retirement are both tied to the success of the same entity, and someone else is making decisions about your retirement.

- **Eliminates Other Options.** Yes, there is a very narrow possibility of reversing one or even selling the non-allocated shares, but it rarely happens. And you know why? Because an ESOP is a ship that's setting sail and it's never coming back to that port. This is not the case for an internal sale (because of a drag-along clause) or a merger or even a traditional sale. Once an ESOP is initiated, though, the company is going to be a mediocre performer; the only variable is time. Technically, you can sell 100% of the shares or just a portion (even a minority interest), but whatever transaction you choose, that will almost certainly be the last one. Or at least the last remarkable one.
- **Later Retirements Are Unfunded.** In general, the ESOP itself is required to buy out departing employees, mainly because the intent of the ESOP is for owners to actually be working there. So if an employee moves on, their interests are repurchased by the ESOP. There's money for this at the beginning, but the money nearly always runs out.

This crisis builds to a head, too, as employees who are considering retirement rush to the exits and exacerbate the challenge. It looks like a fire at a theatre, and the ESOP can collapse on itself. Some ESOPs are not set up that way, but that can lead to another problem: You can't distribute shares to current employees like you wanted.

- **Better Than Walking Away, Worse Than an Acquisition.** The departing (or soon to depart) principal always casts this as a righteous decision to share the wealth and honor the contribution of the team. This same leader wants the sale price to be fair, as you would expect, and so in some cases, they are not maximizing the sale price to an outside buyer. This is not a fault of the ESOP ecosystem itself, of course, but rather just the truth: ESOP sales are financial transactions and not strategic sales that would yield any sort of premium. If you're considering an ESOP and would never sell to an outside buyer anyway, then this doesn't matter. But the point is simple, really: The seller never gets a premium in the sale (though the tax advantages of an ESOP can come close to accounting for this). But this fact—that the ESOP cannot pay more than fair market value—is actually a legal requirement. What's worse is that you, as the seller, will have to carry the note unless you find a bank willing to grant a loan.
- **Expensive To Establish and Maintain.** An ESOP requires a very expensive valuation, onerous advisor fees, yearly valuations and legal filings, etc. The ongoing fees will leave you thinking that you've bought a timeshare that you can never visit. Count

on paying $175,000–$300,000 the first year, and $20,000–$30,000 in every subsequent year.

- **Strands a Remaining Portion.** Nearly every ESOP transaction leaves a retained portion, although you can legally sell 100% of your shares to the ESOP. There are tax advantages either way, but it's very rare for a seller to find any other buyer for his or her shares. This is a separate point from No. 3, above, because it highlights the fact that your payoff needs to come from that original transaction, without counting on any other portion of the firm to sell to the same ESOP.
- **Doesn't Result in a More Engaged Workforce.** I don't want to spend too much time on this, so I'll just suggest something. If you'd like to explore this further, look for peer-reviewed research that's not associated with the National Center for Employee Ownership or other similar organizations with a vested interest: banks, insurers, CPAs, valuation professionals, etc. What motivates employees is a great culture and great leaders, regardless of the ownership structure. And an ESOP doesn't give them any singular control, anyway.

There you go. If you're considering an ESOP, you're almost certainly doing it for the right reasons. But essentially you're giving a 16-year-old a sports car, and 10 years from now—if it's running at all—it'll look like an Amazon delivery vehicle. As good as your intentions are, it's not in the best interest of the people you want to honor. And the modern variant of this, the worker cooperative, is a slightly improved version of the same thing. I'll spare you a missive on that.

What drives culture and financial performance? It's the

leadership and not an ESOP. So to repeat the opening line: The intention behind ESOPs is noble, but the vehicle is flawed.

10: Outside Investor

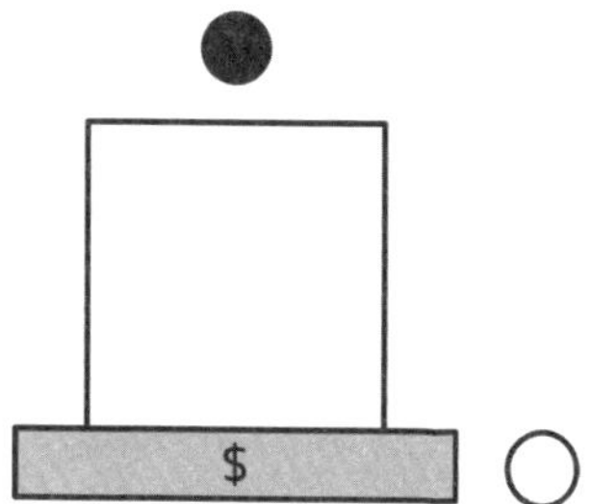

An outside investor purchases (usually) a minority portion of the shares without participating in the active daily running of the company.

This is not the same thing as a loan, which would carry terms and expect a payback over time. An outside investor is giving you money in exchange for a certain percentage of your firm.

When you accept an investment like this, there will always be a clear arrangement in terms of what percentage of equity this investment warrants. Maybe it's $500,000 in exchange for 20% of the firm. Also implicit in that agreement will be an understanding that the investor will always get 20% of the distributions, whenever they happen, but usually they will trust you to pay yourself fairly because there's an inverse relationship between your pay and the amount of distributions—pay yourself more and that additional money isn't available as profit.

However, these arrangements often leave out a method for you to repurchase the shares; here you need to think in terms of two categories:

1. The investor is more of a supporter who doesn't care about the money. They just want to see you succeed and the investment is sort of a like a pocket change bet to them: "I don't really need this money, but it'll help them." And eventually they kind of forget about it. You might ask them for a lot of advice at the outset, but slowly you find your own

footing and there's very little interaction between the two of you.

2. The investor does care about the money. They have a lot of money, but they like a diverse portfolio where someone else is responsible for growing it. They'll ask more questions along the way, monitor your progress, insist on getting financials, attend board meetings, and may even send work your way through their other contacts.

The most expensive outside investment you can accept is the one that you take early in your firm's history. You've decided to leave your job at the mother ship and have quietly secured this outside money. Everything is up for grabs and the risk of investing in your firm is at its highest. A later investment usually comes to fuel a very intentional expansion or to cover some unusual and unpredicted slump in your firm's performance.

Either way, you absolutely need to determine now, before you take it, how you'll reverse the transaction. That doesn't mean that you'll have to stick with whatever both parties decide, because you can agree to renegotiate, but there should be a mechanism. That $500,000 you took for 20% of your firm may now represent 20% of a firm valued at $10M, and it might hurt. That's especially true if the investor is agitating for business moves that you don't agree with.

Sometimes the best way to reverse this is when your firm has suffered a temporary setback or when you can take advantage of when an investor might want the money back for other reasons. This is really about betting on yourself and agreeing on a value that's lower than it has been normally because of circumstances that are having an adverse impact on your firm.

And of course, sometimes the buyer I've described in the first option, above, just wants a return "of" (and not "on") their capital and a bump of some kind that honors their initial faith in you.

If you were an astute investor and had money to allocate, investing in a firm in NAICS 54 (professional service firms) is probably not going to be your first choice, so you really have to design the exit as carefully as you design the entrance to that choice.

Let's move on from these 10 choices, then, and switch back to a traditional acquisition, which is the focus of this primer, and look next at why a buyer might want to purchase your firm.

7

REASONS A BUYER MIGHT WANT YOUR FIRM

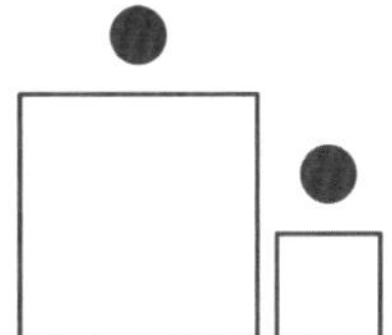

We're going to leave those 10 major options behind, now, and concentrate on a traditional acquisition for the remainder of this primer. I mentioned those so that you can keep your options open in the event that a traditional acquisition isn't in the cards for your specific firm.

There are two reasons for this chapter: The first is to help you slowly build a firm (or shape an existing firm) to the point where it's considered valuable by a potential buyer, and the second is to understand your leverage, which we'll dive into a little bit deeper in a later chapter.

But aside from that, what are the primary reasons a buyer might want to purchase your firm? Here they are.

Vertical Integration

This reason could also be described as purchasing a capability that's easier to buy than build: The buyer wants a capability that you offer. When they've taken a deep dive into their own service offering design, they realize that clients are increasingly wanting to buy two things together. In the marketing world, maybe it's SEM and SEO, because the complexity of each of those offerings means that they should be coordinated for a client.

In a law firm, maybe it's estate planning and probate law. In a nonprofit, maybe it's planned giving and fundraising. In higher ed consulting, maybe it's admissions and development. In consulting, maybe it's strategy consulting and technology solutions. In accounting, maybe it's tax planning and auditing and even IT. In HR, maybe it's the addition of workforce management or even benefits administration.

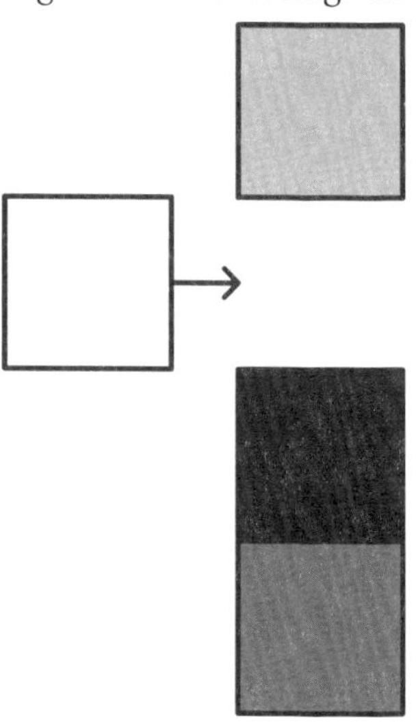

A vertical integration solves a service design challenge by providing more things to the same vertical target.

This is one area where a horizontally positioned firm—because that's more difficult to pull off—can save itself with an excellent exit. (If you aren't sure about some of this terminology, see one of my earlier books: *The Business of Expertise*.) They aren't focused on a vertical, but rather on a very tightly defined horizontal service offering that's applied to many verticals. This can be very attractive for a buyer who is motivated to offer more things to their existing clients ... and to be able to offer what they already do for their existing clients to the clients that the purchased firm is bringing with them.

Horizontal Integration

This phrase essentially means purchasing a competitor, but not necessarily to take them off the market. Nobody reading this book is going to fall under the watchful gaze of the FTC's enforcement division, so it's not really about that. No, the reason they do it is to hasten the process of growth. There's usually a fairly solid overlap between the services that either entity offers and this simply hastens growth, in one fell swoop. Before the transaction, the purchaser has 4% of a given market share; after the transaction they might have 6%, which establishes a "growth story" of 50%.

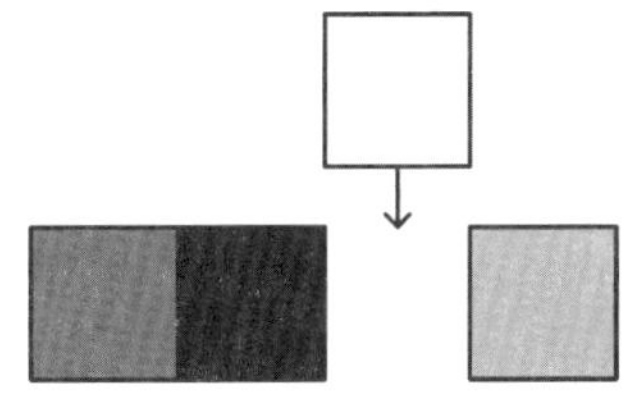

Horizontal integration solves a competitive challenge by targeting sellers who do similar things.

A purchase like this will nearly always be part of a larger plan, and you need to know what that plan is—as well as where the purchase of your firm fits into that larger plan. Horizontal integration is buying another like firm to get bigger, usually, but it can also be a subtle play to fix a client concentration problem. That's next.

Lessen Client Concentration

Let's say I own a firm that has a client concentration issue. In other words, all my firm's work from a related entity, including various divisions within a larger client, or even clients with a common ownership, is 40%.

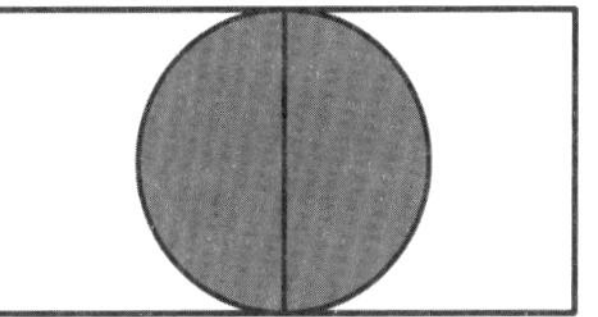

Certain acquisitions (or mergers), by definition, will solve a client concentration challenge because the client is now a smaller portion of the whole.

Two primary risks usually come from such an issue. First, their departure, regardless of the reason, will set my firm back, potentially for quite some time. Second, my firm will slowly begin operating as an in-house department of that client, where it's increasingly difficult to exercise my independent expertise and we instead become more of an outsourced order taker. It's an uncomfortable place to be in, for both of those reasons, and I want to lessen my reliance on that single source of work.

What accompanies that precarious position, often, is an underperforming new business arm. After all, we're really busy and this client is asking for all the capacity we can give them.

Meanwhile, I have several peers with whom I have a fairly transparent relationship, and it turns out that one of them struggles with their own version of what we're facing. Slowly it hits us that maybe we can combine forces. We sit down and note that our big client will drop from 40% of our current entity to 26% of the combined entity. And so a plan is hatched.

I don't want to pretend that this happens too frequently because it doesn't, but we have managed transactions like this. Concentration management is more likely to be a nice benefit of the transaction, though, and not necessarily the primary driver of it. Modifying the story above, maybe one principal is a lot older than the other, and the transaction might be driven by a built-in succession plan—and the client concentration benefit is just the cherry on top.

The standard for defining such a concentration risk (another way to refer to it) varies widely by professional service. In the marketing field, it's generally 15%–25%. In the legal field, it's not considered a concentration risk unless the single related client is larger (40%–50%). So keep in mind that this looks different across the larger professional services space.

Profit Contribution

Some buyers are under a mandate to generate higher financial performance. Their sub-par performance might come from bad leadership, an earlier failed acquisition, changing market conditions, or any other such disruptive event. Most frequently, outside investors and/or an internal board is poised to take more drastic steps if performance doesn't improve.

Primarily, they're searching for a meaningful EBITDA grab that will shift the tide in a pure numbers sense. The topline revenue of the firm being acquired may not be as significant, but two things are true: First, the EBITDA of the acquired firm can make an immediate difference. Second, the synergy of these two firms together will very quickly hit the bottom line in a subsequent wave. That could be from cross-selling, a better sales team, the acquisition of some valuable intellectual property (IP), or dozens of other options.

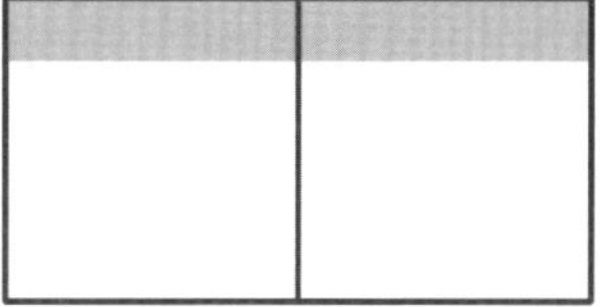

Some acquisitions are driven by the need to quickly add to the profit total or percentage for a specific reason known to the buyer.

Intellectual Property

Speaking of IP, it must be said that there's often a chasm between how sellers assess their own IP and how buyers think about it. But real IP is there for the taking, and sometimes the only way a buyer will get it is if they purchase the source of the IP. This avoids the messiness of licensing it, trying to dominate a market with something you don't own, and so on.

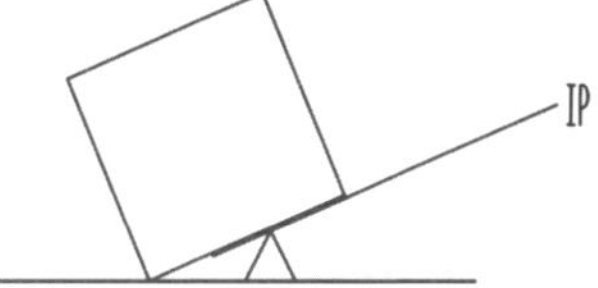

Some acquisitions seek the intellectual property of the seller more than anything else, which they will then use at scale.

You would probably be shocked at the unused IP sitting metaphorically on shelves everywhere. In fact, the majority of patents filed in modern years are abandoned, and there are advisory firms who do nothing more than help the patent owners create new product with the patents that they already own but haven't done anything with (one of our clients does this).

But apart from that, you might have a unique, proprietary

research methodology that a larger firm with a deeper reach might be able to better maximize than you could. This is especially appealing to a buyer if you have demonstrated at least some financial viability to this IP that you've developed—meaning that now it just needs to be rolled out on a bigger platform with more opportunities.

So when you think of IP, think about things all along that spectrum: an electronic device, but also some black box prediction methodology or even a data-driven model.

Alternate Geographic Presence

This is less common in the professional services space, only because we operate in an efficient marketplace, and most of these geographic challenges have been solved. The biggest sports representation firms already have a presence in LA and NYC, and so on. But there are still significant geographically driven acquisitions to be had, and these are often prompted by three very different reasons.

Some acquisitions are driven by the geographic presence of the seller, giving a boost to the buyer's image from the benefits that come from that new location.

The first reason to "buy" a geographic market is to serve clients. Having a market presence that's not three time zones away (or even more) erases the perception that an expert can't service a particular business.

The second reason is for recruiting. You've seen a lot of this happen in the U.S., where a firm that's struggled to recruit tech-savvy applicants decides to open an office in Austin and then realizes that maybe buying a firm that's already there might make more sense. This is especially true if the company requires in-person work environments; otherwise it doesn't matter too much.

The third reason is to pay off a positioning. Most positioning choices have nothing to do with geography, but some do. Say you built a really significant field marketing team in Nebraska but have hit a ceiling on expansion. Maybe you need to be in a major city to reinforce your presence, or to at least remove some question about your location. If you advise clients on healthy food ingredients from a headquarters in Mississippi, maybe you want an office in Portland or Northern California. If you advise clients in the health services space, you will need an office in Nashville. If you are going to make a play in corporate law, you're going to need some attorneys in Delaware, and so forth.

Maybe your firm is in the right place, for any particular reason, and you can play on that advantage.

Subsequent Succession

Time gets compressed as an owner moves closer and closer to retirement. Maybe there have been several false starts with outside buyers, all of which fell through, and without much regret because the more you learned, the less it seemed like a fit. You've had one key employee who really wants to buy your firm, but has no money, probably can't talk a bank into providing enough, and carrying the note yourself doesn't sufficiently derisk your situation to make it attractive. There's even a small group of leaders who want to break all their piggy banks together and assemble a buyout offer, but it's obvious that the group is loosely assembled, in part, for the

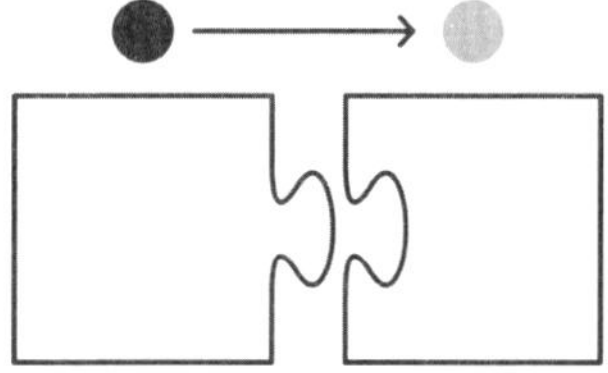

Some acquisitions are essentially "purchasing" a company owned by someone who will eventually be the buyer's successor.

wrong reasons, and the money that they are promising after the transaction closes feels a little suspect to you.

Meanwhile, there's a respected firm in your market. It's smaller and younger, but you hear good things about their work and their culture. The owner is a firecracker new business person and you're a bit tired of that hunt. This other firm thinks aggressively, doesn't have the same retirement horizon that you do, and it kind of doesn't make much sense for you each to fight this fight separately.

It's unlikely that the smaller firm will have the resources to purchase the larger firm outright, but a longer acquisition—disguised as a merger—might very well do the trick, and that's how this happens. A lot of the challenges that must be solved are the same ones that you must solve in a traditional acquisition, but the transaction itself is framed differently and, if done well, can be great for both parties.

Cross-Selling Opportunities

This is the right place to clarify that these transaction drivers are seldom mutually exclusive because everything is about cross-selling. If I'm buying a firm, and they have a great relationship with their clients, and I do something that those clients want, obviously I'm going to sell across the client base they are bringing, too.

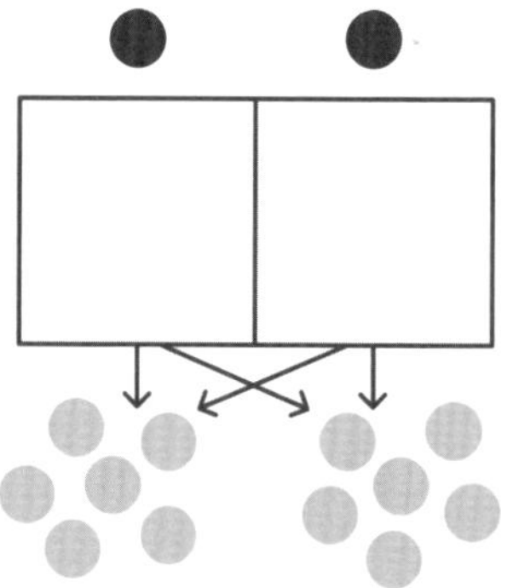

At times an acquisition is driven by the desire for the buyer and seller each to market what they do to the other party.

But there are times when that is the primary purpose, and this happens when the acquired firm already has existing access to the decision makers, even if they are much smaller than the firm doing the acquiring.

More frequently, you'll see this when a much larger firm purchases a much smaller firm, and the price of the acquisition is just the cost of doing business. It's a new business play disguised as an acquisition. One thing to note about this is that the acquirer doesn't care too much about two things: what the firm they are buying does for their existing clients, and the revenue that they generate from that.

To give you a specific example, picture a small firm that has a very high-level executive coaching service. They have one-on-one relationships with some of the most notable leaders in publicly traded companies, and that level of access is almost as important as the work they are actually doing.

A larger executive search firm also relies on that same level of access, only they're delivering different things to their clients. They are helping them find the next opportunity on the polished CV.

Yes, the acquisition is couched as a way to broaden their services to the same market, but what they are really after is the precious and highly engaged subscriber list of that smaller firm, where 7,800 executives eagerly read insights on being better leaders. These are the same people who might also hire an executive search firm at some point in their careers.

Smooth Out Growth Curve

We usually see this in the marketplace when something hasn't gone right. Maybe there's been a downturn in a particular vertical (like travel and tourism during a pandemic), maybe a firm lost a significant client for whatever reason, or maybe some third party's expectations, like a PE firm, haven't been met and we need to fix a blip in the growth curve. Maybe we don't need a hockey stick, but we definitely need a yardstick that points up and to the right.

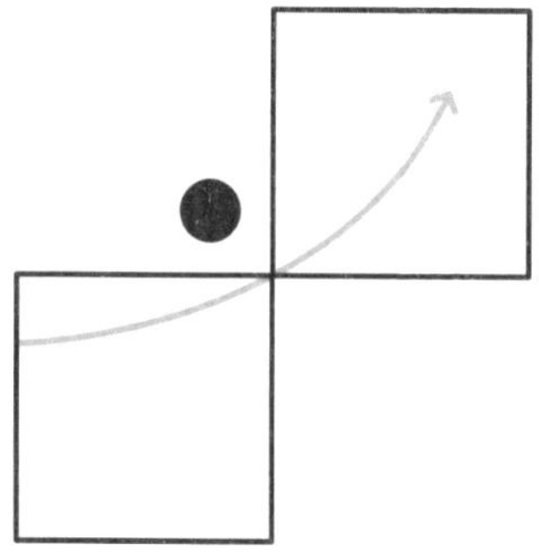
An acquisition may help the buyer tell a better financial story by filling in the gaps that their own performance has yielded.

As long as the cost of that transaction doesn't wipe out the benefit of that transaction, such an acquisition can keep the acquiring firm's growth story intact. The story usually centers around the top-line revenue growth, but not always. It could be for a division of the acquiring firm, the penetration into one particular market, or anything else for which the acquiring firm is under pressure.

Acquihire

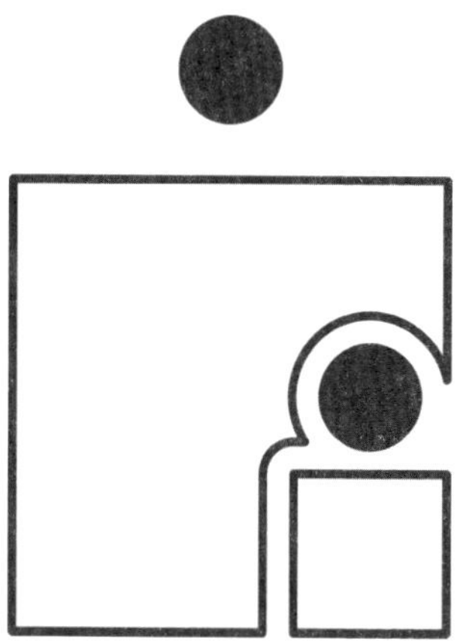
An acquihire helps the buyer add a specific service offering or capacity boost, faster and at less cost than building it themselves.

This is the term used to describe a transaction that's more than hiring all the people employed at the firm but less than a traditional acquisition, and thus the term combines those two concepts.

There are two things that are usually true about the firm being acquihired. First, they do something pretty well, but second, they have a major flaw, and that major flaw is usually business development. Once they get a new client, they keep them; they are really good at what they do, but they struggle to find new clients. They are "head down" in doing the work, but they don't look up to take business development seriously. They probably want to, but it's not a natural instinct and so it doesn't happen.

You'd think this might apply to firms with the opposite problem: They are great at getting the work in the front door but struggle to do the work well. No, that's not usually the target, because those leaders either figure it out, eventually, or they cover for their consistent inability to fulfill those client promises by just finding more clients. The back door is open and clients are fleeing, but just as many new ones are coming in the front door.

The typical acquihire candidate is really good at what they do, but not so good at finding clients to do it for. They are essentially a service delivery firm, just waiting to be placed into a vibrant setting where they no longer need to worry about sales.

So along comes the acquirer who is looking for this capability. They have a well-run firm and they could instantly funnel work to this acquired capability. The "acquired" firm is tired of the sales challenge and just wants to keep doing the work, and doing it really well. But that acquired firm also doesn't make much profit and they have no sales funnel—all they have is an awesome capability. This doesn't justify a traditional sales price, but it's clearly worth something.

What usually happens is that everybody keeps their job, the acquired owner gets an employment agreement (with a possible bump in pay), and they are rewarded for all the clients that stick around. It's not as much money as they would have gotten if they were selling a solid, stand-alone firm, but it's a whole lot better than just jumping ship to the new place.

This is always cast as an acquisition, of course—there no point in demeaning the purchased firm—but that firm is happy with their new life. They can keep doing the work, free of the expectation of something else (usually sales).

An acquihire is harder to find, but much easier to close once you do find them. The trick is to find a firm that's struggling, knows they are struggling, and are finally ready to take another approach without lofty expectations of how much money they'll make in the transaction.

Other Reasons

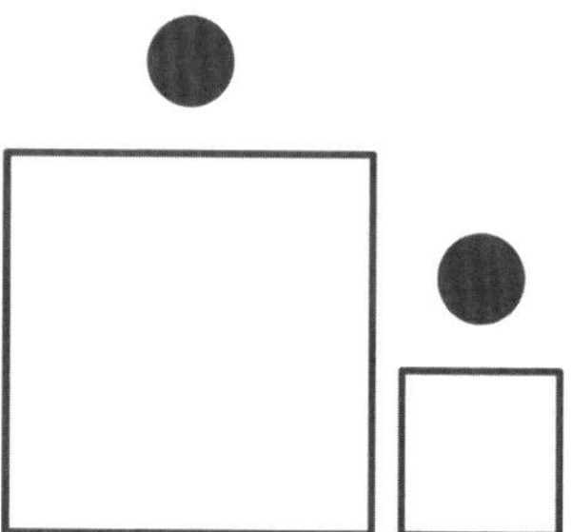

There are many other reasons to buy a professional service firm, but they are rare and will become obvious as you speak with the buyer.

There are other reasons why large buyers acquire smaller sellers, but these seldom apply when purchasing a professional service firm like the ones targeted by this book. The acquiring firm might want to benefit from the net operating losses (NOL) of the acquired firm or they might want to realize the operational synergies that accompany an acquisition, but those are rarely the primary drivers of an acquisition. Instead, they are the nice things that come along with it. As we'll discuss later, though, you need to know about those side benefits so that you can use them, potentially, in negotiations.

On the other side, the very acquisition itself might render some benefits of the acquired firm moot, but it's their job to know about those. Maybe you're a WMBE firm as a female who controls 51% or more of the shares. That hasn't helped you land any business that you wouldn't have landed otherwise, but the buyer of your services welcomes the advantages that brings to them in hiring your firm, but that will no longer be true. This can be handled in multiple ways to retain that advantage, but that'll be the buyer's problem.

If, however, there are "change of control" clauses in your public contracts, it might be an issue for both of you to solve if it introduces any uncertainty in the earnout. These are all issues that will surface later in the negotiations. But for now, it's critical to understand the primary motivation for an acquisition. Not only can you shape your firm to take advantage of that motivation when a buyer comes along, but you can be a better negotiator if you understand all the levers that you can pull.

We're going to step away from this larger-picture stuff and dive right into an imaginary transaction, next, and help you see how and why you might take it on.

8

CONSIDER OPPORTUNITIES & MANAGE DISTRACTIONS

Here are the two extremes we're trying to navigate in this hypothetical: On the one hand, you don't want to be distracted by an opportunity to be acquired so you don't pursue any of them and nothing happens. On the other hand, you entertain any outreach you receive, hoping to find that needle in a haystack.

To avoid both extremes,

- Be open to opportunities.
- Make quick judgment calls about which ones to pursue.
- Approach the first ones as a student.
- Limit your investment in the sale.

Let's take each of these in order.

Be Open to Opportunities

If you are open to opportunities, you listen to conversations differently. Maybe you're grabbing a drink at a bar after a meeting, and the head of another firm you've been working alongside drops a hint. Normally you might just brush it off as someone who's complaining about their situation in a moment more transparent than usual. But if you do this right, you'll have mounted an antenna in a strategic place and tuned into a specific frequency to be alert when those signals crackle to life. Maybe you don't say anything in the moment, but you file it away and then, later, bring it up and ask if there's something to explore.

But the main reason to be open to opportunities is because often the best ones surface organically, apart from an active search that you might be conducting or someone else is conducting for you. You aren't as likely to force those opportunities, which means you're more inclined to walk away when you should.

Becoming distracted by a potential sale is one of the most significant dangers of the M&A process.

Make Quick Judgment Calls

You don't want to get bogged down in chasing something that's not real. I always express this as dating marriageable people, and that's what you're going to look for: signals that this might be good.

Even though all the small talk at the outset helps you gain vital insights into a buyer's motivations and uncovers the real culture of the place that you might join, why do all that unless it's going to actually happen? You'll never know if it's actually going to happen until it actually happens, of course, but at this stage you want to uncover whether or not you even *want* it to happen.

So alternate between the small talk and the big stuff. Find out if they really want to pay for this and if they have access to the money. See if this is "transaction worthy" at the outset, and if it's not, then skip all the nonsense and go on with your life, departing as friends who flirted with an option but made a quick decision to not pursue it seriously.

Approach Early Opportunities as a Student

There are ways that you can prepare (like reading a primer like this or talking with people who have been through it), but there's nothing quite like being in the conversations that might lead to a sale. You'll learn some things about yourself, about your real motivations, about how close you are to ceding control, how attached you are to being your own boss, what you want for your team, and a few dozen other things.

You'll also learn about the questions that a smart (or dumb) acquirer might pose, how your hesitations might be interpreted, and where an outsider might perceive your strengths and weaknesses.

Best of all, you'll model the actual conversations that need to take place. You'll see that the way you thought you should say something doesn't really land, and you'll do a better job next time of articulating a particular position that doesn't create an unnecessary reaction in a buyer.

Keep Your Business Strong

Earlier, I phrased this as not overly investing in the sale. That references the natural tendency for a seller to dream about their new life, with more cash and fewer responsibilities. A new day during which they can bask in the neighborhood crowd admiring that they've "landed the plane" and had a successful exit. You have reached a point where, for the first time, you're willing to let go, and so you play with that new reality in your head.

But here's the danger: If you count on this particular transaction happening, you're quite likely to defer some of those big decisions that your business is really going to need if the deal falls through. One of the most difficult days you might face is waking up to the stark realization that a given transaction is not going to happen, after all, and meanwhile all the big initiatives at your firm have stalled. And now things are even worse than before and you don't have a savior on the other end of the line.

You didn't fix that situation with the problem employee who "quit and stayed" but still controls some important client relationships; you didn't build that new capability that your market keeps asking you for and will go to your competitors to get; your lead funnel is as dry as ever; and your engagement is at an all-time low.

So, be an eager, confident student when a possible good fit comes along, but keep minding the store while you entertain it. If the opportunity warrants it, treat it with the respect that it deserves, but in the back of your head, keep running your firm as if it won't materialize.

9

DEALING WITH AN INTERESTED BUYER

It's a really good idea for you to lead the early conversations, and it's a really good idea for you to bring in a professional, too, at a certain point later in the process. Since you're going to be leading the early discussions, you want to be armed with the right questions to ask, as well as some idea of the answers that you're looking for. We're going to focus mainly on the first part of that equation: What questions should you, on your own, ask a potential buyer of your firm?

Questions To Ask

Why are you undertaking this?

This would obviously be the most basic of all the basic questions in the world, but you've got to pin the answer to the top of your private journal. After you know the primary reason, you can assess how effectively you can solve this problem they are trying to solve, whether it's the right problem to solve, other ways in which you might relieve the pressure they are feeling, and so on. You also need to know this so that you can use it as leverage during the negotiations. If their answer is "because we want a larger geographic footprint and really want to turn up our recruiting efforts on the east coast," then it's going to sound a little hollow when they keep hammering you for your 11% EBITDA: you're still in NYC and purchasing your firm will solve what they claimed as a primary motivation for doing it in the first place.

Why are you approaching us, specifically?

Here you're looking to surface any unfair advantage you might later deploy. The first question is about *what* they are trying to accomplish, but this question is about *why* you might be the right firm to solve that particular challenge. If their answer suggests that you're going to be largely interchangeable with a dozen other firms they might approach, I'm not sure why you'd proceed unless you're just so sick and tired of running your firm that you need an exit, and quick.

The previous question is why you want to get married. This question is about why this person is the right choice. It's all about understanding your leverage and how sophisticated they are in this pursuit. You might be tempted to watch for an unsophisticated buyer that you can take advantage of with your superior negotiating skills, but remember that you'll be working for this fool, later, and it'll backfire. No, you want a sophisticated buyer who knows what they are doing and is looking for a genuine partnership where neither party takes unfair advantage of the other. You're likely going to have to live with this new relationship long enough to get all your money.

It's not just the price and terms you have to think about, but how excited you'll be to be working with this new boss.

Who else are you talking to about an acquisition?

Now, don't fool yourself into thinking they'll ever tell you. That's not why you're asking the question. In fact, you might add an immediate clarification: *I'm not expecting you to tell me, specifically, but I'm wondering what other kinds of firms you are approaching.*

The answer to this will tell you whether it's a helter-skelter broadcast, wasting a lot of people's time, or whether they have a specific strategy. Here's an example of how that might play out: Say you're an 18-person accounting firm in Houston that has historically focused on franchise operators. In addition to your firm, you discover that the buyer is also looking at a 40-person firm in St. Louis that historically focuses on estate planning for wealthier family offices. So unless the buyer can explain how their strategy unifies these different approaches, they just want to grow by amassing eager sellers in a firm that's not going to experience much synergy or even organizational coherence. What you want to discover, when the buyer answers this question, is that they have a very specific target in mind, and that you fit solidly into that consideration set.

Can you tell me about your previous experience in the acquisition market?

Previous experience, successful or not, is not a prerequisite in qualifying a buyer, but you absolutely want to know what experience they are bringing to the table. If it's little or none, be prepared to waste more time answering requests for needless information and getting the order of things all wrong. If their acquisition experience is substantial, be prepared to have your own act together so that you don't get steamrolled by savvy negotiators who've used all the tricks in the book.

But there's another reason to ask this question, too, and that's to surface the people you might want to talk to, openly or behind the scenes, about their experience with this potential buyer. If it was a successful purchase, the buyer should have no problem arranging a conversation with the seller who is now in the midst of an earnout, where they have experienced how fair the buyer has been, whether the promises about the culture were true, and so on. If the acquisition wasn't consummated, you'll want to find out why, even if that means that you verify the information with the firm that didn't walk all the way to the altar.

What You Should Sign

Those are some of the questions, but you'll often be asked to sign two things. One of them you should and one of them you shouldn't—and note that they might both be in the same document.

It's expected and reasonable to sign an NDA. That should protect you and it will obviously protect them. You'll seldom need to ask for any modifications, because these are typically boilerplate documents (personally, I'm not sure I'd even involve an attorney this early in the process, though that's obviously up to you).

It won't always happen, but sometimes a potential buyer will ask you to sign a no-shop clause, too. It simply prevents you from pursuing another buyer while you are evaluating this opportunity, and it further requires that you disclose any approaches that other buyers might make while you are considering this. A no-shop clause is always bound by a timeframe, usually three months, though they can be shorter.

The buyer wants to be sure that they aren't wasting their time (and thus money), but unless there's a breakup fee associated with the agreement, you aren't going to have any incentive to sign it, at least now. The only time you want to sign a no-shop clause is when you, too, don't want to waste time, and you want to send a signal to the buyer that you are serious about this and they should be too. But the time to enter such an agreement isn't now, when the dating is just getting started; it's later, right before everybody is going to take this potential opportunity so seriously that they'll focus on it until it either happens or it doesn't, and there's a lot of time and money that shouldn't be squandered.

Most of the acquisitions we're talking about in this primer will not have a breakup fee, and thus there's little incentive to enter a no-shop period as a seller unless either or both of those things in the previous paragraph are true. You aren't going to get rich if this wedding doesn't happen—you'll just be very sad or very happy.

What Materials To Share

In addition to the early questions you might ask and the information you might decide to share, the potential buyer will also ask for some basic materials from you. Some of these requests are reasonable and expected, and some are premature.

These are the materials that you should feel comfortable sharing if you don't see any red flags in the pursuit so far:

- Ownership structure. Who owns what percentage. You'd want to exclude any small shareholders, especially if it's not yet time to distract those folks by bringing them into the early discussions. They'll likely have a drag-along clause, anyway, and their opinion won't matter in a legal sense, though it will obviously matter later if their approval is central to the deal. You wouldn't even need to disclose actual numbers, yet, but you should be comfortable sharing who the major partners are.
- In terms of financial performance, it's fine to share the topline revenue, the passthrough expenses if those are central to any financial analysis of your performance, and the rough profit. It wouldn't necessarily be necessary to share any EBITDA number that you've already calculated on your own, yet; how and when you reveal that might be an essential part of a later negotiation strategy. Besides, they'll have their own interpretation of that and what you think might not matter as much as you hope.
- Employee count.
- Nature of the work that you do.
- The clients that you do it for. Typically this will be limited to the clients that you have identified on your website and others where there's no downside to including them (in other words, they're impressive), but don't share identifying information about departments or the specific names of your client contacts, at least this early in the process.

In sum, you're giving them enough information to keep the conversation going. They're going to need a lot more if you're expecting an LOI that's specific enough to warrant your careful consideration, but that's later. Here, we're just dating and seeing if it's worth pursuing.

Checking the Social Boxes

Think of your journey at this point as full speed ahead until you see a stop sign. Or rather, 40 mph in a comfortable pace where the talk flows, there's very little tension, and you're just enjoying the casual ride on a Saturday afternoon. Eventually the top is going to go up on the M5, you'll put on a helmet, and you'll be looking to maximize each corner apex, but we aren't there yet.

In that spirit, you want to do some social exploration, and this is best conducted on your own, without any advisors in the way. You can't absorb this stuff vicariously—you have to experience it yourself.

Do it any way you want, but I'm going to give you a specific three-part suggestion to start with:

- Go to dinner at a neutral restaurant. Make it a very nice restaurant, and preferably have a separate back room where you can hear each other but other people can't hear you. Make it a multicourse meal and take your time. Liquor is good (for them, anyway). Look for how much they pay attention versus allow distractions from their devices. Look at who they listen to and include in the conversation versus who they don't pay attention to. Look at whether they let you answer a question or butt in with an interruption. Just get them talking and you'll learn a lot.

- Invite them to dinner at your home. Better yet, accept an invitation to dinner at their home. This is where you learn about their significant others, their approach to family, what their neighbors might think of them, what their choice of pictures hanging on the wall might say about their values, and so on.
- Go to the other person's house for the same thing.

This takes time, but it's a statement about the personal investment you'll be making in each other. It's also laying a foundation for when things might get tougher, in the negotiations or even after the deal closes. You'll understand each other better and empathy won't be as elusive.

The Important Next Step

What I've just described are the important first steps that you should take on your own. Maybe you have an advisor in the wings, but they should not be leading this. Yes, partly it's to save you money, but mainly it's because you need to experience this first stage without any third-party advisor who's interpreting things for you.

But moving forward, it's just as important to have an advisor —as long as it is the right one—as it is to not have an advisor leading things before that boundary.

Everything you've learned up to this point screams, "Yes! This is a good enough opportunity with the right people, who want me for the right reasons, that we should play it out and see where it goes."

But the road has a lot of twists and turns from here forward, and you need someone who knows what they are doing. This is quite possibly the biggest financial transaction of your entire life, and you've never done it before and will likely never do it again, and you really want to walk with an experienced guide.

There are four simple but very good reasons to hire an advisor at this stage. You don't need a lot of legal or tax advice yet—and seeking that input will actually mess things up—but you do need an M&A advisor, and here's why:

- Hiring one is a good sign to the buyer because you are taking it seriously and actually investing in the opportunity. Don't imagine that bringing in an advisor is like clamming up during a police interrogation and insisting that your attorney be present before you do any more talking. No, this is about taking it seriously in a way that the potential acquirer will respect. (If they don't, "there's your sign," as they say.)
- This advisor will speak the language of acquisitions. They'll know what the terms mean, what cadence to expect, what to say when, etc.
- An advisor can shield you from the more emotional exchanges. If you get a question that pisses you off, it'll cloud your mind for the rest of the day. But if the advisor gets that question, they can explain that it's a reasonable request and shouldn't be taken personally.
- An advisor can shield you from the distractions that you don't need, allowing you to avoid that very serious danger of investing so much in a potential sale that your firm flounders if it doesn't materialize.

One last note: Please push back on stupid requests for information.

Unsophisticated buyers, especially, will copy some materials request they find on Google and throw it at you as if you have all the time in the world and have that information at hand. If you get information requests like that, it's a sign of sloppiness or disrespect. Push back, or at least ask if they really need it, before you spend hours or delegate the request so that someone else spends hours on it. Often it's just a reflexive request by someone lower on the food chain who wants to reinforce how important they are in the negotiations. Don't fall for it. We've seen some so ridiculous that they've copied a materials list from an entirely different category. (E.g., the list might ask you to detail your "franchise marketing fee" when you aren't at all a franchise.)

In some cases, you can even say something like, "Hey, how about we swap information? Send us a list of what you need and then give us the same, in turn." Even though they'll laugh and refuse, there's actually some justification for it. Eventually you, too, will need to know who is on their cap table, how financially sound they are, etc. But it's a great way to lighten the conversation and joke about it.

10

KEY QUESTIONS THEY'LL ASK

There's always the odd scenario where someone's just looking to buy location ("We want to recruit near Microsoft and Adobe, so let's have a firm in Seattle") or capacity ("We need more developers and acquiring an entire team that works together well seems like a quicker way to ramp up"). But most buyers are looking for revenue—or they are looking for something else, and using the absence of revenue as a primary negotiating tactic.

So what are the key boxes that a buyer will check your firm against? What does the checklist look like? Think of these as their first questions out of the box. How you answer these determine the offer you'll get. They may care about other things, but the offer will get drawn back to the tried-and-true center and will reflect acquisition basics. Here are the ones you'll see most frequently. (Keep in mind that they already know a lot of things about your firm and won't need to ask about them, like your positioning in the marketplace.)

Profit

This will be expressed as your EBITDA percentage, which stands for "earnings before interest, taxes, depreciation, and amortization," and we'll dive into that in the chapter on valuation. Your EBITDA is usually higher than your net profit, but can't be lower. It's higher when you are given credit for those four things (ITDA), which are added back to your profit number. It may also be impacted by add-backs. EBITDA adjustments are clear; add-backs are not, and you have to fight for the latter.

They might overlook a strict interpretation of this, but they really want 20%–40% (measured against fee after passthrough expenses and not topline). Lower than that range and it's unremarkable; higher than that range and it might seem unsustainable. Keep in mind that any honest buyer is going to normalize your principal compensation to ensure that you aren't subsidizing your net by paying yourself less than expected.

If you know what questions a potential buyer will ask ahead of time, you can begin shaping your firm now.

Recent Trends

Here they are looking at what's happened over the last 3 years or so, but especially the most recent past year. They might annualize a year in which you have completed the first 9–10 months or they might want to look at TTM (trailing 12 months), but it's always backward looking at historical performance.

Ideally, your results over the last 3 years or so should tell a good story. Flat (lack of growth) needs to be explained, and a dip really needs an explanation. Buyers are usually looking for a trend.

Projection of Future Earnings

After looking at what's actually happened, they'll ask you to put together your best projection about the future. Your first instinct will be to smooth out any dips or predict a better near future than the near past has demonstrated, but you need to be very, very careful here. If your projections are obviously more rosy than your recent historical growth might suggest, they will have every incentive to accept them, but only if achieving them gets thrown into the earnout and not the cash at closing. In other words, you're writing checks that might be hard to cash. Don't project anything that you aren't willing to live with.

Not only do you need to explain a recent dip in performance, but they'll want you to explain a recent off-the-charts performance, too.

Revenue Visibility or Quality of Earnings

At times you may see this abbreviated as QofE, which stands for Quality of Earnings. Whatever they call it, it's really a deeper dive into how predictable your earnings have been and thus might be in the future. It's an attempt on their part to minimize the risk of the unknown and accurately predict what's going to happen after they purchase your firm.

This component of their questioning becomes especially true to whatever degree the buyer isn't an insider to your firm's industry. If the buyer is more familiar with the SaaS world, but your firm is more project oriented, you may need to explain how your firm, even though it's served clients on a project-by-project basis for more than a decade, has achieved steady performance in spite of that.

A deeper examination of your revenue, under this umbrella, might ask what percentage of your revenue is recurring, how much client churn you typically experience, your "cost of acquisition" for clients in the first place, how long they typically stay with you, and so on. Be prepared to answer those questions right at the outset. It won't impress them if you say, "Great question. Let me have my CFO do some looking and we'll get back to you on that." No, when the question arises, you'll want to immediately pull up a spreadsheet that has already charted this out. Even if the answer isn't what they are looking for, they'll be less queasy if you've at least worked to understand your business through that lens.

If reading this creates some immediate panic, and selling your firm is just a mental exercise at this point and not something that you're already in the middle of doing, think of the next few years as an opportunity to slowly shape how you craft client engagements. Say you're an accounting firm that performs quarterly reporting work and then yearly tax reporting for your clients. Instead of continuing with an arrangement that yields uneven revenue, maybe your clients sign up for a monthly subscription service that plays out over an entire year, giving you (and the ultimate buyer) a more predictable revenue stream. Or at least one that looks that way.

Inside many firms, we know that a lot of the work is project to project, but outsiders are usually aghast at how we make that work, and so they want as much recurring revenue as possible. Or variations of that, like a contract that's auto-renewing but requires a 3-month cancellation notice. It might be time to get creative and see how you can rethink client arrangements to help a buyer relax, especially if you have plenty of time to rethink this so that your answer to "revenue visibility" questions are more in line with what the buyer is expecting.

Client Mix

Every narrow vertical within the professional services space is different, of course. In the marketing space, a client concentration issue is defined as any single related client source representing 15%–25% of your revenue. For law firms, it's much more forgiving. For accounting firms, it's much less forgiving.

The client will have their own perspective on what's ideal, and their question will likely give you some clues about how they think. They don't see an electric fence that they want to stay far away from, but two electric fences—one on either side—and they want you to stay away from either and walk the middle. In other words, they don't want to see too many clients or too few clients, but even more specifically, they don't want to see clients below or above a certain percentage of your revenue.

One side of this is obvious: If a single related source of revenue is too large, you have a client concentration challenge and your revenue is more at risk because it'll take a hit if you lose just that one client. But they may be equally nervous about the opposite challenge, too: Many small, ankle-biter clients who may be unsophisticated, price sensitive, and unprofitable because of how much handholding they require.

A prospective buyer will be far more concerned with a big client than a bunch of small clients, but you'll need explanations.

Under this category, they want to know who your clients are and what you do for them. How well-placed are you on the client side? How influential might your clients be when they go to cross-sell their services—the things you don't do—to those same clients?

Eventually they'll ask to examine the contracts that you

have with clients, too, but at this stage they just want to get the lay of the land.

Sales Funnel

While you may be proud that your best clients come from word of mouth, referrals, and later career stops from your best clients, a buyer will not be impressed with that. Instead, they want an ongoing system that's already in place, and preferably a slow-burning fire that they can pour some gasoline on. In other words, they want to see if your systems are scalable. They are almost certainly more interested in growth than you may have been. They will assume that you are good at selling; they will not make that assumption about lead gen.

So this question will be all about your sales funnel. How do prospects get dumped into the top? Is there a yearly convention where you hunt for prospects? Do you have a podcast where tens of thousands of listeners know about you and will reach out when they have a need? Do you have a territorial salesforce with a strong history of marketing support and established ways to employ ABM (account-based marketing)? Do you have a CRM (customer relationship management system) that identifies a MQL (marketing qualified lead) and can reliably flip them to a SQL (sales qualified lead) because the reliable buying signals will likely lead to a purchase?

Buyers are nervous about what might change in your firm's performance at and beyond the transaction boundary. But they are most concerned about what will happen to the relationships with your existing clients, and also what will happen to the sales funnel. This is your opportunity to put their minds at ease.

Finally

So that's it. There are a lot of things they don't seem to care about, like your pricing, your sales ability, how many hours people work, your culture, awards, and the nitty-gritty specifics of your staffing.

If you're shocked about anything at this stage in the conversations with a particular buyer, it's how they don't care as much as you do about a lot of things—but how much they do care about a few things you've hardly ever thought about.

When you imagine yourself selling the firm, try to see your firm in the cold, hard light of day that an uninterested buyer might examine it in. They will be interested, of course, but they'll likely be interested in very different things. In running your firm, you tend to focus on the things that contribute directly to your quality of life, like having a great team to manage things for you, for example. Buyers don't care about that. What they care about is how all of your decisions have contributed to a high-performing company and how those things will carry over after the purchase.

It can be quite disheartening to look at your firm like a buyer might because your excuses for subpar performance are going to sound hollow and defensive. So go ahead and step outside your comfort zone and grade your firm's performance as a disinterested judge. For example, you may have all kinds of reasons why you aren't worried about that client that represents a large part of your revenue, but that may not cut it when someone else is being asked to take on that risk.

11

ASSESSING BUYER FIT

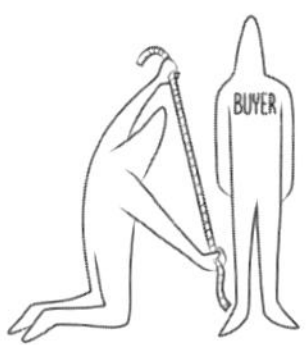

This chapter is the least important one in the book because you're likely to rely on your own instinct in evaluating whether a potential buyer for your firm is a good cultural fit. And frankly, this shouldn't concern you as much as it probably will, but we'll talk about that in a moment.

The hard side of a purchase will come down to how much money they are giving you and when they give it to you. That's kind of it, and you'll have excellent advisors to walk you through all the obstacles as the fog lifts and you have a very clear decision to make.

But the soft side of a purchase is what'll you'll stay awake thinking about at night as you decide to sign the papers or not. What will it be like to have a boss again? Am I even employable? How are my people going to feel about this? Will they even stay long enough to help me reach the earnout targets? Will there be a reputational hit for our brand? Will my competitors scoff and think that some buyer has rescued me from my struggles?

Maybe you're comfortable with the people you've gotten to know on the buyer side, but you wonder about the future as those people inevitably move on. You begin to take on the role of protector: Your people, your team, have come to work for you because of certain cultural promises and now you'll be relying on other people to make good on the things that you've promised, and everything feels very much out of your control at this point.

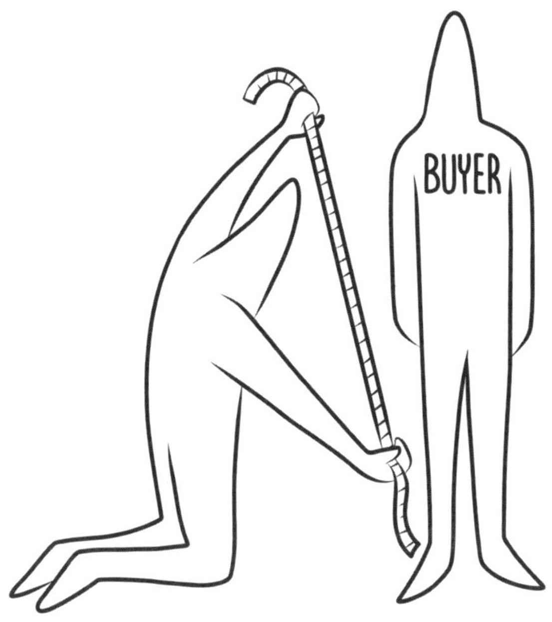

It's not just about the buyer deciding if they want to buy you, but you, as the seller, deciding if they are worthy of your attention.

The Sale Is the Sample

My podcast partner, Blair Enns, is fond of saying this, and I've come to see the impact of this everywhere these days. The sale is the sample. Or, how they deal with you in the negotiations is exactly how they'll deal with you—and your people—afterward. So pay attention to how organized they are, how respectfully they treat you, how they treat the people on their team, the degree to which they accept responsibility when things don't go as planned, how transparent they are, whether you can trust them, etc.

The sale is the sample, and the clearest indication of the type of people you'll be getting in bed with is going to come during times of greater tension when the stakes are higher.

It's going to come when they let their guard down, too. What jokes do they tell or even laugh at? What do their business partners think of them? Are those relationships built on genuine affection or are they mixed with caution and reserve? Do all the things they say to you in the many different settings in which you'll interact align, or are there different stories at different times to suit whatever they are trying to convey?

I can't give you a list of what you should look for, but be very intentional in what you look for, and then very honest in assessing what you see. The sale is the sample and they'll be the same person later as they are now. The trick is seeing that clearly, now, so that there aren't any surprises later.

Be Careful About What You Care About

The suggestion I'm going to make next may strike you as selfish and wrong, but please bear with me and carefully consider your reaction to it.

It's likely that you'll care too much about taking care of your team as you consider whether or not to move forward with a transaction, and that can hurt you. Your unspoken contract with team members is that you'll treat them well, pay them fairly, and give them good career opportunities. But that is not a perennial promise. Just like they can leave you and go elsewhere if you fail to deliver on your promises, the same will be true if the new employer (the buyer) fails to deliver on theirs. You can't control that, and you shouldn't worry about it as much as you probably will.

You may even minimize the challenges you'll face and concentrate on how your team will fare after the purchase closes. Some of that concern is warranted, but probably not as much as will naturally surface. For one thing, your team will almost certainly stick around for at least a year. They'll want to see for themselves if there are more steps on the career ladder, now, and how the benefits might improve and so on. For another, your concern—especially if you've been a good boss—should be centered more on whether you'll get your money and not how your team is going to do.

All the good people who sell their firms will typically care too much about the team instead of focusing on the actual mechanics of the transaction and how solid a deal this is. You're not running an orphanage, and good, solid, employable people will be just that: employable and able to fend for themselves.

You should care, some, because that's who you are. But don't make that the focus. You owe your team a good scenario when thinking about their new bosses, but you can't control everything and you need to begin to step away from the tendency good owners have to make everything perfect.

12

WHEN TO BRING OTHERS INTO THE LOOP

This is always a big question that sellers have: When do I tell all these other people about the sale I'm contemplating? It's a natural question to have because your culture likely values transparency and honesty, and it can feel like you're sneaking around and being less than candid with people. There's no one clear answer, either, so just develop a general approach to it and think on your feet as things unfold.

Tell people too early and you risk a lot of unnecessary drama if nothing materializes. Every person you tell raises the likelihood of word slipping out to someone who doesn't need to know. Tell people too late and they'll feel disrespected and unheard, and they'll fight the transaction.

Keep in mind that the nature of the transaction will impact when (and how) you bring others into the loop. For example, your clients will consider a merger less of a concern than an acquisition. Similarly, a 3-year earnout eases people's minds about the culture because they assume that you aren't going to screw yourself by joining an entity you hate working for.

The groups I'm going to cover next are listed generally in the same order in which you might bring them into the loop. That particular order is much clearer than the timing, which is going to depend on how things unfold organically.

One difficult challenge for sellers is when to tell others that you are now in discussions with a possible buyer.

Significant Partners

Absolutely no conversations should take place without full disclosure to all major partners. What comprises a "major partner" is subject to discussion, but think of it generally as anybody who's involved in all the big decisions.

An owner who controls 5% of the stock, but who is rising in importance and is an active part of the ownership group, is far more critical than a 5% employee who was gifted that stock to keep them from leaving.

This group should be told immediately, after the very first indication of interest from an outside party. And of course they will be intimately involved if you are engaging an advisor to initiate a search for you.

The only reason you might keep a significant partner in the dark is because you are going to dump them as part of the transaction, funding a buyout as part of the negotiations. But make sure you're willing to face the prospect of them finding out in other ways before you agree to have these discussions behind their back.

Minor Partners

Minor partners—any partner not included in the first group—are next. The ownership agreement or bylaws will almost certainly include some sort of drag-along clause, so technically how they feel about a transaction isn't material, but that's obviously not true from a practical standpoint. They have the ear of certain clients and certain members of the team, and their tacit approval—even if it's not enthusiastic—is in everybody's best interest.

Even the buyer will care about this, so much so that they'll certainly confirm each partner's endorsement before the LOI, and then the purchase agreement, is autographed. Each partner, minor or not, is likely to have an employment agreement, and so everything is going to surface anyway. You might as well do it in a way that doesn't make anyone feel unseen and unheard.

This should occur right after the opportunity seems real enough to actually pursue.

Board of Directors

Many small firms don't have a board of directors, but if you do have one, they should be brought into the loop next. After all, this is precisely why you have a board of directors: to give you objective, somewhat external advice. And some of them might even have acquisition experience in a prior life, or at least might know of good advisors if you don't already have them lined up.

This group should be included as soon as you decide to take active steps to pursue an acquisition.

Key Management Team

The next group that should know about the possible transaction is the key management team: the five or eight people who help shape the company's direction. You aren't really asking for their permission, but rather trusting them to be reliable stewards of inside information.

Here I want to make a distinction between the people you trust wholeheartedly and those you don't. At any given point in a company's history, you can expect to find some members on the management team who are in a transition. You want to replace them but haven't yet done so. Or there's a question about how long they will stay around or where they loyalties lie. Or maybe someone is going through a difficult personal issue (midlife crisis, divorce, family health crisis, death of a close relative, etc.) and now just isn't the time. The point is that it's okay to not treat each management team member the same.

The timing of this notification is not really set in stone. The latest you'd inform this group is probably immediately before signing an LOI. Use your judgment, but they'll need to know as soon as it'll be difficult to hide it from them—and/or when you need to know what they will think about the possible transaction. When the buyer is taking a tour of the facility and meeting people in the company, you don't want to be lying about why that's happening.

But also keep in mind that these are the good people who will be running the place while you navigate the easier conversations and the more difficult negotiations, so it's a balancing act. You want to treat them with respect by keeping them informed, but not so in the thick of things that they can't do their job of running the firm and keeping the performance solid enough to fulfill the promises you've made in the projections.

The buyer is also, at some point, going to want to know about this team, and maybe even meet with some of them. They want to know if that person will stay and provide some of the continuity that's important to a successful transaction. Some individuals might be important enough to warrant a special arrangement to lure them into staying, and so the buyer will want to make their own assessment of cultural fit and overall competence.

Employees

The rest of the team will find out immediately after the purchase agreement is signed and not before. There might be a few people who are brought into the loop earlier, but that's the exception.

This last internal group is where most of the pressure will lie because you can't really be confident that they'll keep the secret, but it's also hard to keep it from them for the entire 3–5 months while the process unfolds.

Clients

Clients are next. You'd only tell them when one of these things is true:

- You don't want them to find out in another way.
- You need to know if they'll stick around after the transaction closes.
- The acquiring firm insists on speaking to them.

On that last point, this should happen, if it happens at all, very late in the process. Almost as the very last step before the glorious signing of the purchase agreement. You'll get a fair bit of pressure about this, too, as the buyer will want to make their own assessment of the security of that client relationship, but you must hold them off until the very last moment.

Vendors

Vendors might be curious, but they aren't going to care. They might actually be excited about the prospect of getting more work from you, or, of course, they might wonder if they are going to be replaced by the buyer's favorite vendor. Either way, it's honestly none of their business and you shouldn't waste too many brain cells worrying about it.

World at Large

This would occur last, and would typically be delivered through a press release, a pop-up on your website, and so on. It would never happen until the transaction has closed and it'll be fun. The only thing to think about is how it's framed, and whatever you say won't be entirely true. This is the proverbial "resigned to spend more time with their family" statement—never true and quite disingenuous.

But when you frame a purchase as "excited about playing on a bigger stage," there's going to be a lot more truth to that, regardless of the nature of the transaction.

You'll probably want some media training to manage this final stage of bringing everyone into the loop, or at least do some role-playing with someone on the team who can ask the tougher questions.

Next comes updating your LinkedIn profile and a big celebration, of course, after all of this hard work.

Who does the work? That's where assembling the team comes in.

13

ASSEMBLING THE TEAM

There's not a lot to talk about, here, but there are a few important points about who should be on the team and when to bring them in. You might have the right people on the team—but bring some of them in too early and the entire acquisition might blow up in your face.

We can think about this in six categories, largely in the order in which you involve them. Trust me, though: Give this chapter to one of these advisors and they'll disagree vehemently about when they should be brought in. But they will be wrong.

Trusted Advisor

This is someone who is not a professional, per se, but someone who can keep a secret, can ask the hard questions, isn't afraid to piss you off, offers their observations even if they aren't entirely welcome, and whose judgment you trust.

It would obviously include any partners you have in the business, who can't be kept in the dark anyway, but it could also be a life partner, a business mentor, and so on.

This is not the person who knows all about M&A, even though they might have been through an acquisition or two, but someone who knows you and what's best for you.

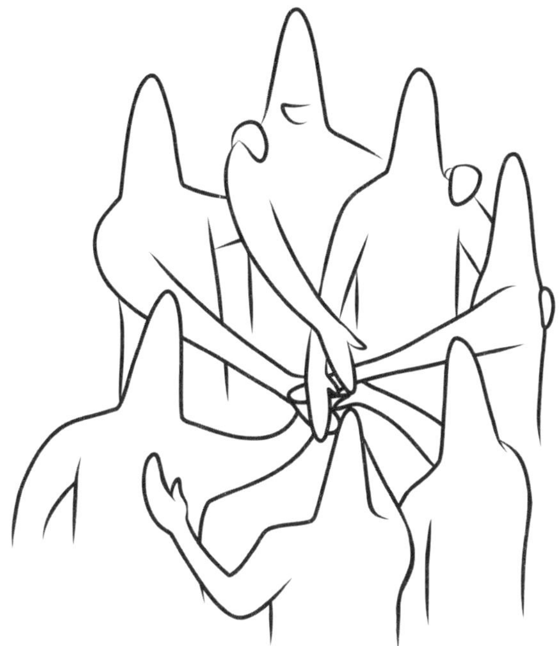

Who you add to the team, and when you add them, is an important part of a successful outcome.

The only warning I'd sound here is this: Identify this person to your advisors and don't let them come in at the last minute, clear the table, and make you start over. That sort of disruption will really piss off your advisors. Let everyone know about this person and assure them about how measured they are and how respectful they'll be about the other professionals that you're going to involve.

M&A Advisor

This is not usually a lawyer or an accountant. This is someone who advises buyers and sellers (ideally both) on a regular basis. It's what they do for a living. This person knows the ins and outs of a transaction and they can see around the corners ahead before you can. The next chapter dives deeper into this role, but it's always the first person you need.

You might bring them in to help you navigate a deal already in hand, at a minimum, or you might engage them earlier to conduct the actual search, vet the possible buyers that surface, and lead you through the entire process. They will be by your side from the very beginning through a week after the earnout at the celebration dinner.

We are M&A advisors.

Tax/Financial Advisor

This person should be on call very early in the process. They will know all about your type of corporation, how to present financials in a professional way that'll give the potential buyer confidence, how to answer questions about where to find all the add-backs during a valuation, and how we might structure the deal in a tax-advantaged way.

The one warning I'll give you, here, is to listen to their guidance, but do not structure the deal primarily from a tax perspective. There will be room for those discussions, later. Just like a dentist looks at the teeth of everyone they meet, an accountant sees everything through a tax lens, and that sort of myopic view will bog the discussions down. You'll be digging into the details while many of the big issues aren't even resolved yet.

Have them on call, and establish a strong working relationship between the advisor and the accountant, but let the advisor lead. Good advisors will usually prefer to work with your existing accountant, too, and will know how to respect their work and not step on their toes. When it unfolds like it should, the finance person will quickly appreciate the role that the advisor plays. They'll see the bigger picture, but they might also know how to push back on your ideas.

Attorney

You will always need a good attorney on your side, and sometimes you might already be working with a tax attorney who can do both of those things.

This shouldn't just be the attorney that helped you collect money from someone or who helped you craft an employment agreement. Instead, they should at a minimum have strong experience in business contract law, and even better would be someone with experience in M&A transactions.

If you make a hiring mistake in putting together the team, the two most likely mistakes you'll make will be in choosing an M&A advisor and choosing an attorney. We'll look into what makes a good M&A advisor in the next chapter, but there are really good attorneys and really bad attorneys.

I don't mean that so much in terms of their knowledge of the law and how to apply it, but their personal demeanor. Good lawyers are smart, articulate, self-aware, and not immediately antagonistic and adversarial. Bringing any attorney into the process too soon—and this is particularly true if it's one of those bad ones—will piss off the buyer and derail the entire process. It'll leave a bad taste in everyone's mouth, including your own, and things will take forever to resolve because of all the grandstanding and snippy email exchanges.

Just don't do it. Get a great one. If you already have one of those, the M&A advisor will always prefer to work with yours.

The M&A advisor is just joining the team you already have. But if you don't, find one or ask for a referral.

That's it. That's all you're going to need except for small things around employment, benefits, and so on.

But there are two other partners you might bring in, later in the process but before it closes.

Change Management Consultant

A lot might be changing, and soon. Your team will be a little shocked and they'll have lots of questions. You may be great at guiding everything through the next rough waters, but a change management advisor can really help.

This person would advise you on what to say and how to say it, and they would be available to the team to smooth the way and establish good two-way conversations.

Comms/PR

The final advisor, if you don't already have this on staff, would be someone to manage the public communications to the right parties at the right times. We've covered when to bring others into the loop in an earlier chapter, but a PR and communications professional might be really helpful, depending on how large a transaction this is.

If you're a small 10-person firm only known to your family and the industry you serve, it might be just as simple as an email and some changes to the website. But the bigger the transaction is, the more important it is to handle this really well. Don't let your competitors use the transaction against you.

Let's look next at one of those six advisors—the one who will be leading this process and corralling the entire team for your benefit: the M&A advisor.

14

WORKING WITH AN M&A ADVISOR

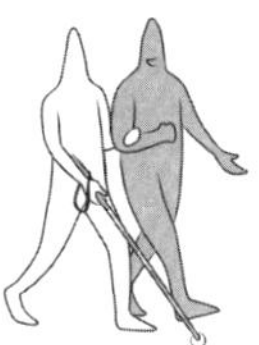

Think of the M&A advisor (hereafter, just "advisor") as the person working most closely with you, the conductor guiding the team on your behalf and making sure that everyone is pulling in the right direction.

All of the advisors described in the previous chapter should have your best interests at heart, but the M&A advisor will see the bigger picture and translate all of these things for you. The advisor will rely on the deep expertise of each of the other members, partly from their training or their experience or even their unique understanding of how things are done in that geographic area with its own laws, but they will bring it together.

Two Primary Roles

The advisor really has two primary roles, sometimes separate and sometimes together:

- Search
- Negotiation

If you bring a potential buyer to the table, or one just drops in your lap, you'll hire an advisor, probably, to help you do two things (other than helping you decide if it's worth pursuing, obviously): first, maximize the opportunity and second, minimize your personal risk (often called "derisking"). They help you get the most they can for your business without destroying the good relationship you need with the buyer—while anticipating problems and having solutions for them.

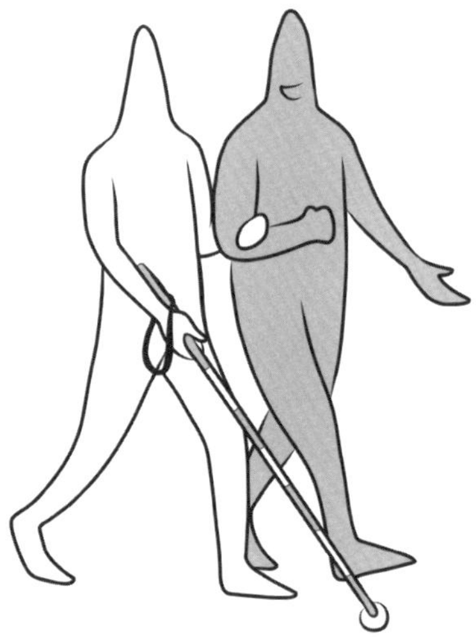

If you have the right M&A advisor, they can help create a much better outcome for you, the seller.

But say that you enter the M&A world and you don't have a buyer, yet. In that case, you'll engage an advisor earlier in the process to surface a buyer for you. It doesn't always have to be the same person, but it usually is. Anybody who is good at conducting a search will be skilled at negotiating it for you, but the opposite is seldom true; many skilled deal closers don't have the interest or skills to conduct a search.

What a Search Looks Like

A search process is always going to take at least 3 months, and might extend up to a year. If the search hasn't been successful over a year or so, it's probably best to call it off and assume that one or both of these things are true: the market is in a unique place where activity hasn't been robust, or there's something about your firm that isn't sufficiently appealing to that market, even though other firms are being bought and sold.

The search will begin with a fairly intense process of getting you ready for that sale. This will include discussions where you and the advisor get on the same page about what's motivating the sale, how to talk about any of the weak spots that a buyer might see, and then a prospective sale package that includes the history of the firm, its strengths, the reason for the sale, representative work, the price, and the terms. It's very much like what a realtor would do before staging your home for potential buyers to tour, except there's a lot more at stake...and life must go on during the process. In other words, you're still living in the house, and with an entire team around you.

The advisor will at times step outside their unique point of view and simulate the buyer's point of view. Since you'll have many conversations with the buyer without the advisor present, you'll be more confident and well-prepared if you've practiced that dialog..

Once the firm is ready to go to market, the advisor will start talking to potential buyers. It's likely that the advisor will have hundreds of buyers in a database. This is the gold that sets the advisor apart. When an advisor primarily represents sellers, it's just as important for them to nurture relationships with buyers, too. These buyers have been very specific, often, about what they are looking for, and so it's natural to reach out to them, first, to gauge their interest in this specific opportunity. Or maybe their plans have changed recently and now this firm that the advisor is representing is a good fit. (These same buyers might flip the process and engage the advisor to find a firm for them, too, in which case the search process is reversed.)

If the potential buyer is interested, the advisor will secure an NDA. Even though the buyer won't have the sale packet in their hand yet, they'll know the name of the firm being sold, because it'll be identified right there in the NDA. This points to another reason why the advisor needs to cultivate good relationships with potential buyers, in advance of an engagement, to build a trusted relationship where the process remains confidential. The advisor might tell you about the opportunity before this exchange, but usually they'll only bring you in the loop after the potential buyer wants to learn more, ensuring that you aren't distracted from running the firm.

The potential buyer and advisor will have several conversations about the opportunity, the potential buyer will bounce it off their internal team, and if it seems worth pursuing further, they'll ask to speak to the seller. The advisor will bring you up to speed and explain what's unique about this possible buyer, and off you'll go for a private conversation. (Refer to Chapter 09 "Dealing with an Interested Buyer," to review how to conduct this conversation.) Or either party might want the advisor to be in that first call.

Assuming this goes forward, and assuming that you didn't include detailed financials in the earlier packet, the potential buyer will see those next.

And there will be countless conversations between the possible buyer and the advisor, with the advisor keeping you updated and getting answers from you to questions that they can't answer on their own.

After gauging interest from their proprietary database of potential buyers, as well as listing the firm and advertising it, anonymously, to tens of thousands of email subscribers, the advisor might commission a specific search just for your situation. This can take a few weeks and is usually done by a staff member.

And then, of course, the advisor will share the opportunity with their network of other advisors to find the appropriate interest.

One note I'd like to make, here. There are advisors and there are listing services. A listing service throws you into a pool with dozens of other firms for sale. Once you sign with them, about the only effort they make is to send a broadcast email out to their list, which includes thousands of unqualified buyers who are mainly tire kickers. Your firm will be easily identifiable via an internet search, and the "advisor" will overwhelm you with dozens of unqualified buyers. These would-be buyers will get your information packet to pour through, often via an automated NDA process that just lets anyone access it. And if that's not bad enough, they will then pressure you to take a deal that's not in your best interest because they want to get the commission and move on to the next sale. Please don't confuse an M&A advisory firm with what's more like a listing service. Even if they wanted to help you negotiate the deal (and they don't), they don't have the experience to do it well. They're staffed with junior salespeople who sit on the call with you and offer no leadership or pushback, and you'll wonder what you're paying for, you'll feel very alone, and you might very well step into a deal that you'll regret over the entire earnout and when you have to go back to work because the earnout potential vaporized.

What Deal Negotiation Looks Like

This chapter separates the search from the negotiation because not all advisors do both. Some pretend to do both but are really only a listing service. And some advisors don't conduct a search for you, but are skilled in negotiating a deal. You find a potential buyer on your own, take it to them, and they'll do their best to maximize your opportunities and minimize the risk.

Negotiating deals is a real skill. Not only does the advisor need to know what they're doing, they need to be aware of alternative ways to achieve goals when they hit a roadblock, they need to be firm but not so antagonistic that the buyer wants to deal directly with the seller instead, and they need to surface all the areas that need to be negotiated in the first place.

Negotiation is an art and it's not the subject of this book. If you're looking for a taste of how an advisor you might hire will work on your behalf, pay attention to how they craft an arrangement with you before even getting started. Is it transparent? Simple and clear? Fair to both parties? Confident? Knowledgeable? Patient? How they interact with you is how they'll interact with a buyer on your behalf.

Negotiation itself can look like an endless cycle of getting close ... and then starting all over ... feeling like we have a deal ... and realizing that this might all fall apart. The advisor will learn about who you are as a person and will tailor their communication style and completeness to what you are looking for, and each of the advisor's clients are different. Each time an advisor works with a potential buyer on your behalf, the process will become a little bit smoother because they'll know more about you and what questions possible buyers might ask.

The relationship you're going to have with your advisor will sometimes look like a hate sandwich: It starts great as you get excited about the prospect of moving to the next chapter of your life, you'll hate some of the middle parts during which the advisor will level with you, and then you'll love the advisor again when you get the check ... and slide into the earnout period.

The advisor, if you hire the right one, is a professional. They care more about their reputation in the long term than they care about their relationship in this one engagement with you. They are not going to do something that hurts their standing in the greater marketplace by talking you into a deal that's not in your best interest or trying to trick a buyer into something. That's exactly the kind of advisor you want, but that also means that you won't always get your way. Get over it.

How long will the entire process take? The biggest variable is the search, which is hard to predict. But once a real buyer is in the picture, negotiation might take 4 weeks at the very least, but more like 2–3 months.

How Advisors Get Paid

This is all over the place, quite frankly. It has to do with whether you're getting different things from the same source, like a valuation, a search, and negotiation.

A valuation is probably $2,500–$10,000.

The search is often based on what's called a "success fee." In other words, they don't get paid unless they find a buyer and the transaction closes. The commission can vary, but 4%–10% is the typical range, and sometimes this is based on a sliding scale (smaller percentage for a larger transaction).

That commission can be based on the entire value, but it seldom is. Partly because it's hard to calculate a commission on an earnout that hasn't yet materialized and can't really be predicted, but also because you kind of want your advisor to have an incentive to shift as much of the sale price as possible to be paid in cash at closing.

And then there are often some flat fees that are paid at the outset of the search. This ensures compensation for all the work of preparing your firm for sale and shopping it around, even if a buyer doesn't materialize. Note that this is actually in your best interest as a seller, too, because if the advisor only gets paid if the firm is sold, they'll have too strong an incentive to shove a deal down your throat so that they haven't wasted all that time up until that point.

What will the advisor be negotiating? Well, a lot of things, but at the top of that list is your firm's value, and that's what we'll look at next.

15

UNDERSTANDING HOW YOUR FIRM IS VALUED

The title of Chapter 7 was originally "Reasons Why a Buyer Might Want You," but then I decided that such a title might sound too personal and changed it to what you see here. The original title reminded me of a scene where someone you wanted to date in high school turned their nose up at you and how that might have made you feel. So I changed the title, but there is some truth to the original version.

One of the things you'll face, when you get your valuation and settle on an asking price, is this: "Really? This is what I put 18 years into this firm for? Sure, it paid me, but I was assuming that I was filling some sort of pot at the end of the rainbow and it's discouraging to see this number." It'll be hard for you to separate the valuation you receive for the firm from how that makes you feel as an individual.

A Valuation Isn't Personal

So it really helps to think of a valuation as an objective exercise that's coldly analytical, even though—as you'll see—there are clearly judgment calls (and a later chapter will walk you through how you might contest the valuation).

A valuation is designed to assign an "objective" (the adjective) value to your firm. I say "objective" but the truth is that there can be many "objectives" (the noun, plural), too. You can bring those two concepts together by noting that each valuation is done for a specific purpose. I can promise you that a spouse might think differently about the purpose of a valuation in a divorce settlement (share one-half of a lower number) versus selling the entire firm to an eager buyer (some percentage of a higher value).

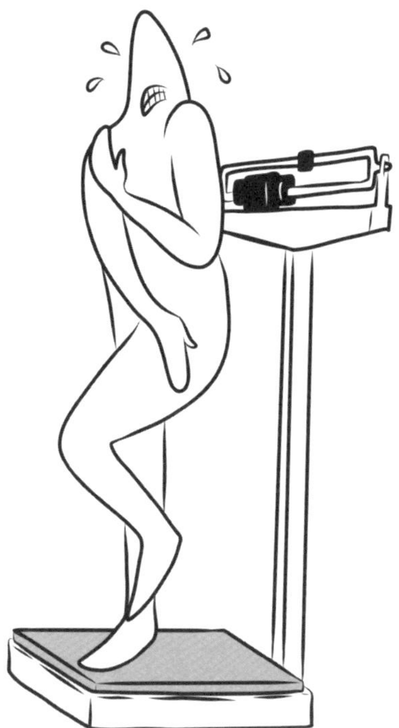

The valuation process can feel needlessly personal, but you shouldn't view it that way.

But while the purposes (or objectives) of the valuation might differ, the methodology is always transparent, and so it must be defensible if it's going to carry any weight. Besides, valuation experts are math nerds who tend toward the analytical side of things and they care a lot about their reputation. Here, though, we're going to think about an objective valuation that both parties might dislike, which might be a sure sign you're on the right path.

Price vs. Terms

First, though, a word about the relative importance of the established value of a firm and the related terms under which that transaction will be consummated. We always say, "terms are more important than price" and that's a restatement of that same concept.

Valuation theory (for professional service firms in the $5–$50M range, which this primer targets) always starts with a multiple, so that's where we'll start, too. And then we'll discuss all the other factors that impact the final valuation.

Here's something to help frame all of this before we dive into the deep end. Think of the larger transaction as something that's composed of the valuation and the terms. So think something like this:

Valuation + Terms = Transaction

In this chapter, we're covering the major factors that will impact the valuation. There are many other factors that might impact the terms (how long you plan to stick around, what the buyer's goals are, etc.), but these will be covered later.

And to expand this further, the valuation itself is composed of book value and goodwill. Book value (also called equity) is essentially the difference between everything that you own and everything that you owe. So on the plus side, you'd include cash, savings, accounts receivable, the depreciated value of your hard assets, etc. On the negative side, you'd include credit cards, loans, line of credit, accounts payable, etc. The difference between those two is your book value.

There's little dispute around book value. It is what it is. It's a hard number that can easily be verified. That forms the foundation of a valuation, and no valuation can drop below that number, simply because you can close the firm, tidy everything up and—bam!—you have that book value without finding a buyer.

Valuation theory, though, is about what's built on top of that book value, known (unfortunately) as "goodwill." The calculation of goodwill rests on many formulas and assumptions, and that's primarily what we're discussing here. There's a small section in this chapter where we come back to book value, and of course there's lots to explore regarding the terms of the sale, but here we're focusing mainly on goodwill and the role it plays in setting a price for your firm. With that understanding, here's how that would look:

Goodwill, because of its name, can be difficult to understand, as one element in the transaction that also includes book value, as well as the terms the describe how the purchase price is delivered.

Foundation: the Multiple

There are many reasons to buy a firm, and some of those have very little to do with the financial side. But a valuation uses various formulas to assign an actual dollar value to the firm. That's where it starts, and if the purchase is a money play, the final valuation won't stray too far from that resulting number. If there are other reasons for the transaction, it might—or a buyer might even use the valuation to beat you up in the negotiations, even if the purpose of the acquisition isn't about money.

We are going to pretend that it's purely a financial transaction in this discussion of valuation, though, and we'll start by defining what a multiple is. Multiples were first developed and applied in the 1800s. The idea was to come up with some standardized way to compare relative assets. The assets being compared were companies, and the standardized method of comparison was the extent to which each company generated profit. That's basically the core of valuation theory: how to compare the relative degree of profit. This was such a core concept that multiples became the primary way of setting the value of firms in the 1900s, through the court system and economic journals.

Let's pause for a second, because this should strike you right in the heart. When you are selling a firm, the buyer wants to know, primarily, how successful your firm has been in creating profit. The buyer doesn't want to buy your firm because it's provided you a job, reflected in your salary, but whether or not it generated a profit after all expenses were paid, including your compensation. The buyer will care about how much you paid yourself because they want to make sure that you weren't subsidizing that profit simply by paying yourself less than expected; otherwise, the buyer just wants to know how profitable the firm was.

Over time, financial analysts have developed more sophisticated valuation methods, moving away from multiples to consider things like DCF (discounted cash flow), but those are more appropriate for firms in industries that require heavy indebtedness, and thus a tighter focus on returns after servicing that debt.

The target of this tome is smaller professional service firms, however, where debt is not a traditional consideration for ongoing operations. There may and likely will be some debt, but servicing that debt is usually a very small part of the firm's financial performance. This is important, because any valuation methodology more appropriate for a manufacturing environment with huge capital requirements (machinery, equipment, facilities, inventory, etc.) will not usually be as relevant as a simpler and fairer valuation based primarily on a multiple.

It's better to not think of multiples as the result of some mathematical formula that tells us how to value the firm you are selling. No, multiples are simply historical. They are based on what other firms like yours have sold for. They fall within a narrow range, and the valuation expert needs to assign a specific multiple based on factors unique to your firm, but the range itself is only applicable to firms like yours that have sold in the recent past.

That narrow range of the multiple is based on the NAICS code within which your firm is categorized. (NAICS, or North American Industry Classification System, is a set of standardized codes that describe business sectors and industries; they're used in collecting and analyzing U.S. economic data.) Your firm probably falls under code 54XXXX, where the four numbers after that larger 54 category (which denotes professional services) delineate whether you are in architecture, engineering, legal, consulting, marketing, etc. For marketing firms, for instance, that multiple range has historically been 2.5x on the low end to 12.5x on the high end, with the vast majority falling somewhere in the 4.0x–6.0x range.

Keep in mind, though, that these multiples are applied very specifically. For instance, they are applied to EBIT or EBITDA and not net profit. Several years are included and then averaged together, and not always in a straight average but a weighted average. Principal compensation needs to be normalized, any unusual expenses need to be subtracted (these are called "add backs"), and so on. We'll cover those shortly.

Where does the information come from when assigning a multiple? There are many sources, but primarily:

- Experience in doing valuations and defending them.
- Networking with other valuation experts and comparing notes.
- Public databases of completed transactions (i.e., DealStats).

The simplicity of the multiple is wonderful, but people focus on it too much. We're often asked what the going multiples are these days, for instance, and we'll answer the question, but it doesn't really mean anything. It's like asking someone how much their friend weighs, without knowing if they are male or female, how tall they are, and where the weight is distributed. It may be a great place to start, but it doesn't mean all that much in isolation.

But it is where a buyer will start, and that shines a light on one of the most fundamental purposes of a business: how profitable is it. That may not matter to you as much as it will to the buyer, but trust me when I say that your profitability is definitely going to be in the spotlight.

Let's look at the other factors that will play a role in how your firm's value is calculated.

Revenue vs. Gross Profit

Say you hire a firm to pave your driveway. Their two primary expenses will be materials (the hot, smelly black stuff delivered in a truck) and labor (the people doing the work who get that stuff all over their boots). There are many other expenses, like the equipment they use, their advertising, and so on, but the profit they generate generally comes from only two sources: markup on the materials they purchase specifically for that job and their skill in arbitraging labor.

Anything that a firm purchases on behalf of a client will usually be marked up at some known percentage. This reflects the fact that they buy in bulk and get better pricing than you could, know what to buy and when, and so on. They are rewarded for this knowledge with their markup, as well as being rewarded for the risk of buying materials for a job where the customer stiffs them on the bill.

They also employ a bunch of full-time workers. Essentially they're saying: "Hey, we'll employ you into the indefinite future. We'll give you this much money per year, broken up into smaller payroll periods, and it'll be our job to sell your labor—that "time" we buy in bulk—to our customers. And we'll have to make some profit on this because there's quite a bit of risk in employing you. We'll often keep giving you a paycheck even if we haven't secured enough work, we'll make some hiring mistakes, and so on."

So the paving company's income will come from two primary sources: pass-through expenses that are marked up, as well as arbitraged labor.

But firms in the professional services space don't rely on pass through as much as other industries. In our space, a marketing firm might incur the cost of digital advertising, a law firm might use outside expert testimony, a tech firm might have expensive software licenses or hosting fees to recoup, and so on.

The hard costs of those outside expenses is calculated carefully, using each narrow vertical's customary way of doing it, so that a valuation can be performed. What we're left with, after subtracting those external expenses, is essentially gross profit, composed of the profit generated from those two sources (markup of pass through + markup of labor). Here's a marketing firm example:

Total revenue: $9,000,000
Less pass through: $1,000,000
Equals gross profit: $8,000,000
Minus overhead: $6,000,000
Equals net profit: $2,000,000

Focus for a second on the source of that $8,000,000 gross profit. If they mark up their pass through expenses of $1,000,000 at 20%, they make $200,000 from that activity. That would mean that $7,800,000, the remainder of their gross profit, comes from arbitraging labor.

The profit that this firm is expected to generate is measured against the $8,000,000. In fact, some firms are glad to run expenses through the company and bill them out at cost. Others have very high markups. These are all reflected in the expected multiple of that narrow NAICS target, but it's always calculated against the gross profit and not the topline revenue. That's not true in all industries with intensive capital requirements, but it does apply to the market we are addressing.

Normalized Principal Compensation

What the top leader earns in a multibillion dollar company, apart from stock options, has no material impact on the company's performance. It's just too small a number to matter. But that's not true in a small professional service firm, and so valuation experts (because they know buyers will care) will take this into account. If you are underpaying yourself, you are essentially subsidizing whatever profit there is. Conversely, if you are overpaying yourself, you should get credit for that extra amount in the bottom line.

What's an appropriate amount to pay yourself? Just like multiples, that's based on industry standards, and usually that amount is tied to the size of the firm, measured either by employee count or revenue. It's just common sense that you'd expect a principal to make more money if they are leading a bigger enterprise. More skill is required and there's often more personal risk attached to that role. Even if there isn't, a buyer will often need to determine the replacement value of that executive, and it's unlikely that someone would take the job without the requisite market rate compensation.

So underpaying yourself will hurt your valuation since a qualified valuation expert will take that into account. As we'll see later in our discussion of terms, there's another reason to pay yourself fairly, because that will make it easier to vie for a reasonable employment agreement during your earnout. It's harder to argue for that amount, whatever it is, if you've not required it over all these previous years. And you can't say that you pull the rest from profit, because you can't count that profit twice. It's either profit or it's unrealized compensation, and if you want to claim some of that profit as closing the gap with your low compensation, it must be subtracted from what we previously thought was free and clear profit.

Pattern Consistency

Here the buyer is trying to determine the degree to which future performance is likely to match past performance and how to explain any abnormal changes.

What a buyer is looking for, essentially, is predictability. If the valuation is to be based on the last 3 years of performance, and each year your revenue and gross profit and net profit have incrementally increased by 20%, you'll have no trouble arguing that next year should continue that performance boost. But if year one and year two have essentially been flat, but year three shows a 40% increase, we have to understand why. Was previous flat performance abnormal and now we're seeing the firm perform as planned? Or were the first two years typical and all this extra performance in the most recent year is easily explained by one large client whose needs kept juicing your performance? (Especially if that client just happened to learn of you rather than coming to you as a natural result of a strong marketing plan.)

Weighting the Time Periods

Before we talk about how the periods are weighted, we need to talk about how many periods there are that matter, and how to even define a period.

Valuations are calculated in yearly units, but those units might not correspond with a calendar year, or a fiscal year, if that differs in your case. In other words, the last "year" might be comprised of the last 4 trailing quarters. Or better yet, the last 12 trailing months.

It wasn't uncommon in years past to look at the 5 previous years of performance, and that's still standard practice in some industries, but not in the small professional services market. That's because things change so much more quickly. More firms are founded and flounder in any given year, the economy changes quickly, competition is never static, technology has a massive impact, and even legislation doesn't create as stable an environment as in the past.

Nobody really cares what happened at your firm 5 years ago, but they are going to care what happened over the last 3 years. And even within that 3-year timeframe, what happened in the most recent year will count far more than what happened 3 years ago. That's the best way to introduce the concept of weighting. So if the valuation is looking at the last 3 years, they very well might not be weighted equally, at one-third each. You might start by weighting the last year at one-half the valuation, the next year back at one-third, and the earliest year at one-sixth. And then you rework the weighting decisions to account for all the unique situations of each target firm.

As we're seeing, here, valuation is a science, but it's also an art.

Unusual Expenses

These are commonly called add backs. If your net profit dropped during a particular period during which you incurred unusual expenses, it would be common to "add those back" to the bottom-line profit number, since they were subtracted from revenue before net profit was calculated. That's why they are called add backs.

Typical add backs include a rare lawsuit that incurred significant fees, a rebranding that you may do every decade, the distraction and extra cost of a move into a new facility, a very rare case of a client going out of business before they could pay their outstanding bills, etc.

It's fair to take these into account, but be sure that you can make a strong case for each one. The buyer is not going to just let you do it without examination, and your objectivity and transparency is important if you want them to trust you during the negotiations—heck, even after the negotiations, during the earnout.

Client Concentration

The phrase "client concentration" refers to what portion of your revenue comes from one related source of work. While it's true that fewer, bigger clients deliver much greater efficiency in revenue generation, they also represent a greater risk should one of them leave. Losing a 2% client isn't the same as losing a 20% client.

Companies whose shares trades on public stock exchanges regularly warn investors of those risks (and others), because they are real. Each industry, and even each category in professional services, will have different standards for a client concentration challenge. When determining that risk, the buyer will consider:

- How long the client has been on your roster.
- The nature of the arrangement: project by project, or under a longer recurring revenue arrangement that might even auto-renew or require a longer cancellation phase.
- Whether you are embedded in different departments, each of which operates independently.
- Any likelihood that your client would be acquired, in which case everything is subject to change.

Even if you have a client concentration challenge, it may not hurt your valuation. And as the seller, you'll want to make a case for this. You would put yourself in the buyer's shoes and argue something like this: "Yes, we have a sizable exposure to one related client entity. I understand that you don't want to purchase a firm where a significant portion of the revenue is at risk. So we could discount the valuation to reflect that risk, but what if the client *doesn't* leave and in fact we continue growing? Then I have no way to recoup my loss from selling the firm for less than I should have. So let's build your legitimate concern into the terms, instead. That way, if we don't lose the client as we work together, I'm fairly compensated, but if something catastrophic happens, you will be protected."

Sector Trends

Valuations are great as long as the world marches along without any major accelerations or decelerations in particular sectors of the economy. We all saw how travel and tourism took a dip in early 2020, while SaaS and ecommerce grew faster than normal, until they didn't. The influence of AI on content and software engineering has to be considered. Elections. Media mergers. Major rulings from the Supreme Court. Heightened regulation. Chevron doctrines.

A valuation always captures the value of a firm at a discrete point in time, and the larger trends will be used to determine a multiple and many of the other factors that influence a valuation.

Book Value and Working Capital

Everything we've been considering so far in this chapter relates primarily to how we should interpret P/L (profit and loss statement, or income statement) performance in calculating a valuation, but there's more to this.

Picture two firms with identical financial performance, client makeup, etc. But one firm has a much thicker balance sheet than the other, composed of more cash, a bigger spread between their AR and AP, or higher depreciated value of their furniture, fixtures, hardware, software, etc. Shouldn't one of those firms present a higher valuation? The answer, of course, is yes.

That fact largely won't matter if the transaction is being cast as an asset sale, because the seller will typically retain their balance sheet, collecting the AR, paying the AP, selling the inventory via a formula in the closing documents, and then keeping all that's left.

But the balance sheet will come into play in two cases:

- When it's a stock sale, which would typically include any value represented in the balance sheet.
- When calculating how much working capital the buyer requires the seller to include in the transaction, whether it's an asset sale or a stock sale.

Stock sales will typically require a certain amount of working capital and let you keep the rest. Buyers don't want to pay dollar for dollar for any operating cash they don't need.

Asset sales may not require a working capital infusion, but if they do require you to fund that, it would frequently be pegged at 2 or 3 months of working capital. The closing documents, which you'll be able to review far in advance, may include very complex formulas. These are applied later, after the transaction closes, and more information has come to light. Have all the clients paid? Were there any expenses that we didn't know about? Was the work in progress for a certain client agreement estimated at the right line in the sand?

For now, concentrate on your P/L, and then keep the right amount of working capital in your business. There's actually an optimum amount, as well. Too little and you can't respond to changing market conditions. Too much and a) you leave it unprotected (a corporation protects what is *not* in the corporation) and b) you may not feel an appropriate amount of pressure to make larger decisions as quickly as you should.

Then, if that's how you're viewing your balance sheet, there won't be a working capital deficit to make up or excess capital to drain before the transaction.

Buying a Valuation

The typical valuation for a firm inside the target readership of this book costs $3,000–$12,000. But if you're paying less than $5,000, you may not be getting a thorough one, or the person doing it is using the process as a loss leader and they'll make it up in a later service that you'll be pressured to buy.

The valuation should come with a written document and an oral explanation. Any valuation expert will also defend it to an opposing party, at least in writing and by phone, and maybe even in person. If there is substantial time required in defending a valuation, it's customary to pay additionally for that work, including any travel expenses.

Some valuation models might also allow you to update it in the future. You likely won't be in a position to make any different decisions about weighting or multiples, but you can always let the oldest year roll off, update the new numbers, and see what happens. This is one more reason why you should understand every part of a valuation.

And let me say this: Do not buy a valuation that you don't understand. Just like we're told to not make any investments that we don't understand, don't buy a valuation that someone can't explain and then defend to you. Trying to wow you with obscure language is just lazy rather than impressive. More on that in a minute.

How Purpose Influences Outcome

One small note here about the role of *why* you're getting a valuation and how that might influence the outcome.

First, you have to ask yourself if it's even okay that a valuation for one purpose, say a divorce, might be different than a valuation for the 100% equity transfer to an engaged buyer. The same can be true, for example, if you want to facilitate the sale of 10% of your firm to an internal buyer who may eventually become your successor, and that person doesn't have any money.

I think we *should* be careful with this concept and be intellectually honest. There's an inside joke in valuation work, and that's that both sides should be disappointed.

The guidelines for this are, just honestly, based on ethics

and reputation. But in the bigger picture, the true value of a company cannot be pegged to a specific price, but rather a range. Let me illustrate that with a specific example.

When you commission a valuation of your firm ahead of a possible acquisition, you want to know how much it could possibly be worth in a way that both maximizes your proceeds in the sale but doesn't make the buyer walk away because the number is so out of touch. Once you arrive at something workable, then you wrestle with the terms of that sale: how it's actually paid to you. The price is somewhere in a range, and the buyer is pushing it down and you are pushing it up.

But imagine that you run the firm on your own and your spouse has their own career. A divorce, for whatever reason, is going to happen, and there's no prior agreement that specifies what portion of the firm each of you own, which means that you each likely own one-half. You, as the remaining principal in the firm, are not going to fight for a high valuation, but rather a low one. And your spouse will push for a higher one within that range. In fact, one of the arguments that might be used against you is a recent valuation that you had done, for a different purpose, which shows a higher amount. You'll be hard-pressed to declare, then, that it's worth less.

But the purposes are different. The risks are different. The terms are more likely baked into this valuation (you don't get along, your soon-to-be-ex might not care about your continued prosperity, etc.). It might be the same range, or it might not, but you're each pushing in different directions because you have different goals.

This is why valuation is both an art and a science. How else can you justify the extreme—yet still valid—methodologies around valuation theory? For goodness' sake, some operating agreements stipulate that the value of the firm is pegged at book value, with no goodwill attached. Others specify a multiple. Some have no formula, but instead rely on a shotgun clause where one partner can offer to purchase the interests of the other, and the partner receiving that offer can accept it ... or flip it.

Good valuation work takes the larger context into account.

Valuation Transparency

This brings us to a very important note in this very long chapter, and one I've touched on briefly above. It's common to hear financial advisors—at least the ones who embrace their fiduciary duty to you, the client—say something like this: "Don't invest in anything you don't understand." A financial planner might come to you and suggest that you should take a look at Section 8 housing, and by God they should be able to make a case for it, and you should leave the conversation understanding how it works, what advantages there are, and where the drawbacks could bite you. The same with any other investment.

In those conversations, there is the expert (your advisor) and there is you (the client trying to get up to speed). You'll likely never understand all the nuances of that recommendation, but you should understand it well enough to, in turn, be able to explain it to your neighbor. (This is known as the Feynman Technique or the Protégé Effect.)

The same thing holds for valuation theory. If you understand basic math, the valuation method applied to your firm should make sense ... or you should be nervous. Here's what you're looking to avoid:

- A valuation method applied to your firm that's more appropriate for another sector, like a cashflow method that was designed for a capital-intensive and debt-laden manufacturing environment.

- An accountant who looks at things strictly through a math lens. This is what happens when they don't understand valuation theory but subscribe to a valuation service, answer the prompts (which are 100% mathematical), a multiple is pulled blindly from an NAICS chart, and the 45-page report is generated as a PDF. And then when you ask questions, they stammer. What you've just purchased is the application of a software package that the valuation people subscribe to, and they can't explain the underlying theory behind it.

If you do not understand the valuation, it could very well be that your advisor doesn't, either. So insist on normal language that resonates and keep asking questions until you're satisfied.

Let's take a deeper look at this "goodwill" that we've referred to multiple times.

16

THE ROLE OF GOODWILL

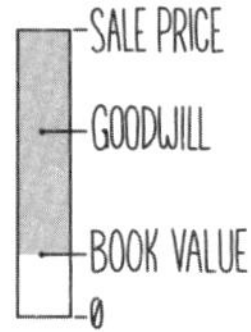

This is a separate, but very short, chapter because there's one component of valuation theory that's always confusing to people who are newer to the discussion. Part of that confusion comes from the term itself: goodwill.

Outside of valuation theory, goodwill is defined as "friendly, helpful, or cooperative feelings or attitude." Trust me, nobody is going to pay you for that, and negotiation about the value of your goodwill might not be all that friendly or helpful or cooperative!

No, in this world, goodwill is the term used to describe the intangible value of your firm, measured as the difference between the valuation (what someone might pay) and its fair book value (what you'd have if you just sold all the assets). So think of it this way:

To play that out, let's simplify with an illustration of value for a sample firm. Say that we're going to ignore all the valuation factors (weighting, compensation standardization, etc.) and just focus on assigning a multiple of 4x to their EBITDA. The firm's revenue is $2M, their net profit is $300k and their

EBITDA is $400k. We apply the 4x multiple to the $400k and the valuation we get is $1.6M. There will be many other factors that are built into the final price, too, especially some assumptions around working capital from the balance sheet, as well as the depreciated value of the actual fixed assets (computers, etc.).

Let's assume that it's a stock sale and the seller is retaining the balance sheet and the corporation (that's what a stock sale means), but that the buyer is requiring that the seller include $200k in working capital to fund the ongoing needs of the firm.

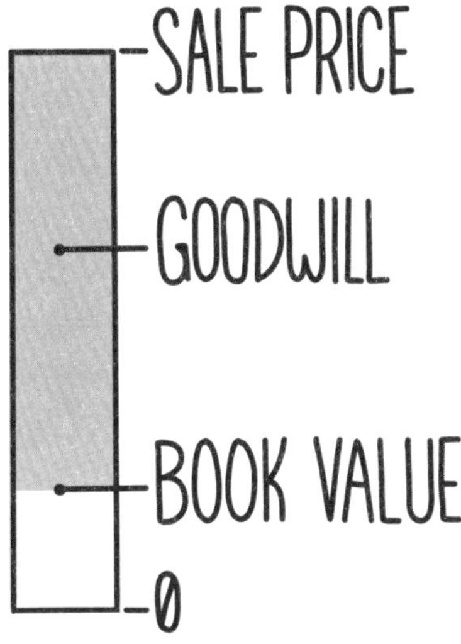

Goodwill is a confusing term, but it actually represents the bulk of what the buyer is purchasing.

The book value of the firm being sold is $200k and the firm is being sold for $1.6M. The goodwill of that firm is the difference between the two, or $1.4M. This goodwill is going to be booked on the balance sheet of the purchaser, and eventually it'll need to be depreciated. It's an intangible asset because there's nothing that you can pick up and touch (like furniture).

But even though you can't touch it, there are still real assets all wrapped up in goodwill: a brand's reputation, its client relationships, customer loyalty, and maybe even some proprietary process or technology that helps to generate that ongoing stream of money.

So you can think of it this way: book value + goodwill = valuation.

What's unfortunate about the terminology is that it screams "soft asset"—when in fact that's actually the primary thing that you are buying. Even though you can't touch it, it's very real. But because you can't touch it, we have to have a valuation methodology that approximates its value.

When we got married, my wife had more on her balance sheet than I did. I basically had nothing and she had about $4,000. I didn't marry her for the $4,000 (although that's how we bought our first car, a very ugly Impala that was hand-painted with a brush in unspeakable green). I married her for all the intangible things. Sort of the goodwill. The ongoing relationship, the conversations, the mutual commitment, our kids, our partnership through struggles, and so on. The entire "marriage" was the sum total of our (as in, her) "book value" and the "goodwill" of what a relationship meant.

So don't get confused by goodwill. It's simply what someone pays for your firm, minus the book value that's included.

17

CONTESTING THE VALUATION

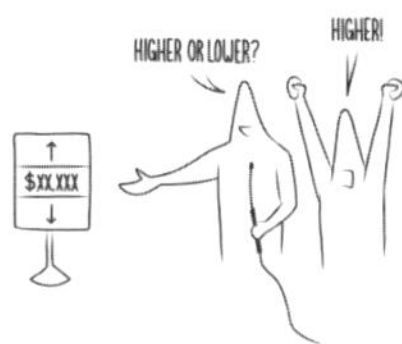

After you receive your valuation, you'll almost always think it should be higher. If you've commissioned the valuation, don't necessarily think that the professional who produced it will buckle to your pressure to make it higher just because you're paying for it.

As a professional, that person will know what it's like to defend a valuation to the opposition, and they might have even had to do so in a legal setting (we have done both). So you can't move them off their tentative conclusion without solid arguments. If nothing else, they will take pride in their reputation as an objective outsider, a reputation that naturally comes with disappointing some clients. You can try, of course, but don't expect them to be an order-taker who just does your bidding. Even in trying, you'll start a good conversation where you might surface something that should have been considered. At the least, you'll understand valuation theory better after you hear their explanation.

At the same time, you can expect the buyer's valuation to undercut what your firm is really worth (keeping in mind, of course, that terms are usually more important than price, so all may not be lost). In this scenario, you'll need substantive arguments to build a consensus for a higher price. It's your job to give them the support they'll need to justify a higher price to whoever is controlling the purse strings behind the scenes on the buyer side. While there's primarily science undergirding a valuation, the algorithms are not ironclad and can be questioned.

And remember that the buyer—that other party—is not obligated to accept your valuation, and you'll see that if you compare a transaction like this to the last time you bought a house and went to a bank for the loan. In that transaction, there are two people deciding what your home is worth.

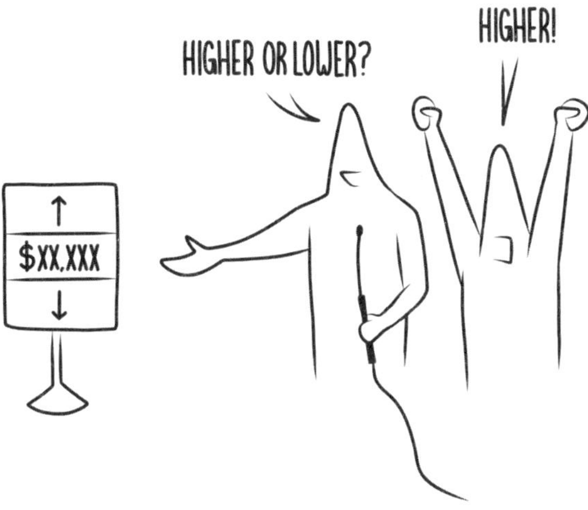

There are legitimate ways to push back on a valuation and ask the expert to reconsider specific elements of it.

The first party is you. You look at this house and you compare it with the other houses that you've looked at. You really want it and you think it might be worth a certain amount. You haggle a bit and agree with the seller that you'll buy the house for this amount, whatever that is. But the offer you make to the seller is contingent on getting financing, and that's when the other party also needs to decide what that house is worth.

The bank will enlist their own appraiser—who works for them and not you—to get an independent, objective opinion of what the house is worth, and they won't care what you think the house is worth or what you offered. All they care about is covering their own ass if you default on the loan, in which case they'll be stuck trying to find another buyer who will then pay them back for the money they loaned to you. And the bank is going to assume that the second buyer will only pay what the house is really worth, and not what you thought it was worth.

In that scenario, the bank will do their own "valuation" of your new home. In the same way, the buyer will do their own valuation on what your firm is worth, and they don't much care what you think it's worth. If a deal is going to get done, their valuation will need to come close to yours.

You might disagree with the number that the bank comes up with, and you'll need to arrive at some cogent arguments to sway them off that number.

Here are the typical ways you might craft that sort of argument, divided into the major categories, in your quest to legitimately push back on a valuation. Obviously you could combine these, and of course these are not exhaustive. Missing from this list are all the unique motivations that the buyer might be bringing to this possible transaction, which you can use to your advantage.

In a sense, this chapter is the inverse of Chapter 16 "The Role of Goodwill", but we can simplify some things and make it easier to make your case.

Argue For a Higher Multiple

This is the most obvious place to start because it's the multiplier and thus has the biggest impact. For example, a change from 4x to 5x will increase the valuation by 25%, so it's really significant.

But assigning a multiple may be the most expert-laden element of a valuation, and you'd better be prepared to defend it. Just like a league-high salary can reset the floor for a positional contract in any sport, you'll have to argue that such a comparison is a) normative and that b) you fit the same model. In addition, be sure you understand the context thoroughly. Your arguments here can range from average multiples for your NAICS code to a recent transaction that's outside the norm but similar to your situation.

Here's an example: Until recently, near-shore software engineering firms attracted deficient multiples, but one transaction of a 126-person firm involved a multiple of 12x, resetting the market where similar transactions were in the 4x–6x range. The buyer was a new holding company entering the field that needed that firm for their portfolio, but the deal set a precedent that other firms might use.

Claim More Add Backs

When doing a valuation, the advisor is rightly looking for one-time expenses (or income!) that than can be discounted to make the firm look more valuable. In Chapter 15 "Understanding How Your Firm Is Valued" you read about the usual things that qualify as add backs, but maybe you can be creative and find something that the valuation missed. Just a warning: The add backs we hear people argue for are hilarious and it's hard to keep a straight face at times, but there are legitimate ones that bear discussion.

Fight For Compensation Credits Outside Salary

There's some overlap between this point and the previous one, but it deserves its own category. The perspective that feeds this objection is the sense that you are paying yourself way more than it looks because of all the things you are charging to the business: your personal travel, your car, a business retreat that the business helps pay for, a phantom family member on payroll, a big life insurance policy, etc. It's an odd argument because you are essentially giving an IRS agent all the proof they need in an audit to justify removing that business deduction and instead categorizing the expense as a personal benefit subject to personal income taxes.

Here's the thing to keep in mind: You really only have a point if your excesses are more excessive than all the other principals in your shoes. Most everyone will run their auto expenses through the business, and the business might even purchase their vehicle and pay all maintenance and operating expenses. So it won't be unusual to do that and therefore you won't be able to legitimately claim that you're doing something different. But say that the business isn't spending a typical $1,000/month for your auto, but instead the business leased a Lamborghini for you. Well, then you might claim that the new owner of the business (the buyer) won't be expected to do that, and so the delta between the $1,000/month and your stupid decision to lease the Lambo at $3,000 should be credited to your firm's performance.

It falls a little flat to say that you're a bigger cheater than everyone else because it requires a stout belief in your own exceptionalism. But sometimes it is true. Just don't be ridiculous, because you aren't comparing your compensation with a staff member's but rather yours against other principals, and most of them are doing the same things you are. The most ridiculous argument of all is to add back all the executive comp because "the buyer won't need any of us." That's a bridge too far, but there are often (other) good arguments in this category.

Minimize/Ignore a Down Year

Unlike in valuations from a decade ago, nobody cares what happened at your firm 4 or 5 years ago. The focus is almost always on the last 3 years, and those years are not typically weighted evenly. So, what if your next-to-last year wasn't great? You can argue that it should be excluded. "Officer, I don't normally speed, but ...." And you actually may win this argument, but you'll need some tight explanations: a worldwide pandemic, a big downturn in a particular industry, the unusual loss of a significant client, etc.

At the same time, be prepared to explain why you didn't prevent this from happening in the first place and what safeties you've installed in the management structure and reporting that'll make it less likely to happen in the future.

Reclassify Nontraditional Income

Sometimes you can include nontraditional income in your business performance and justify it. There are isolated instances of this all over the industry, but the most recent broadly relevant scenario in this category was the unearned PPP (paycheck protection program) funds that firms received in the U.S. While it was widely welcomed as a survival tool, it wasn't actually needed (in most cases). Should that be recognized as income or should it be ignored? In this category you'll also find one-time windfalls from the sale of assets, subleasing income, equity conversion, etc. They are all judgment calls.

Keep the B/S; Sell the P/L

In a previous chapter, we talked about how some buyers will insist that the seller fund certain levels of working capital even if the transaction is structured as an asset sale. But say that the buyer's interpretation of your balance sheet doesn't match yours. Maybe it's the firm's art collection, leasehold improvements to the building that you own and will be leasing to the new buyer, the collectability of debt, the perceived future value of some enterprise you've recently begun, etc.

You can keep the rich balance sheet and just sell the income statement (P/L). Our methodology always accounts for anything on a balance sheet, but there are many valuation exercises that pay scant attention to the value of a balance sheet and instead focus on an income statement. The typical balance sheet (in a healthy company) accounts for 20%–30% of a valuation, though, and so if you haven't received full credit for yours, this is an area where you might concentrate.

Move the Focus from Price to Terms

If a buyer is balking at the price, maybe just assuage their concern by agreeing to terms that derisk the situation for them. Instead, you assume the risk of hitting certain goals. Bet on yourself, essentially. In this case, maybe the buyer has come to you with an offer of $14M, one-half at closing and the other half over a 3-year earnout. You're fine with the length of the earnout, but you think the firm is worth $18M. You could agree to the same $7M in cash at closing, and build the other $11M into the earnout.

Or the opposite might be true. The same offer comes to you for $14M plus a 3-year earnout. Maybe you can live with the price, but you don't want the terms. You'd instead angle to keep the price the same but agree to a 2-year earnout for the rest, plus an option that would be mutually agreed upon at the close of the 2-year period. Or something like that.

One mantra that you should always keep top of mind is this, and it's the one that we've repeated many times in this book: Terms are usually more important than price. On top of that, keep in mind that buyers usually focus more on price than terms, and thus you'll be more likely to influence the terms than the price.

Omit the IP

Have you developed some unique advantage in your work that depends, largely, on an algorithm or a software product or research methodology or even a plug-in? And the buyer is dismissive of the value of that asset?

Call their bluff and exclude it from the transaction. You could even give them a lifetime, nontransferable, nonexclusive right to use whatever it is, either for free or via some licensing agreement, leaving you to market it in other ways and even fund the further development of that product.

Depending on how substantive the IP is, you should probably set it up as a separate entity, anyway. That'll make it easier to track the development costs—and the income—and a side benefit is that it would not be subject to any legal action that might attend your company as a whole.

Give the Buyer a Tax Incentive

You can always agree to a taxation exception to favor the buyer. One of the concessions you can make in the purchase is to keep the purchase price at a reasonable level and enter a deferred-compensation arrangement in exchange for a noncompete, a focus on new business post-sale, or whatever. This can throw you, the seller, into a higher tax bracket (income tax vs. capital gains tax), but it makes those "payments" deductible to the buyer, effectively lowering the seller's taxable income. This has to be managed carefully and properly to comply with IRS rules, but it's a common approach to give the buyer a real benefit that they otherwise would not have. It's also a way to keep you on payroll, if it's important in your financial planning to still participate in the health insurance and/or retirement plan.

Sell the Hockey Stick

"We're on the edge of exit velocity," you might claim. This argument is designed to reverse the stock market axiom: "Past performance does not predict future performance, but in our case the future won't just match the past, but will exceed it!" You'll obviously need to make a powerful argument to support this, but here's an important warning: Be ready to see a shift in how the purchase price is allocated, moving away from cash at closing and throwing more potential into the earnout. Never make projections that you aren't willing to stake the overall purchase price on, as a savvy buyer will happily give you enough rope to hang yourself.

Play the "Strategic Purchase" Card

You can claim that it's a strategic purchase, which is a little different from the previous point. This is the Hail Mary of valuation objections. "You aren't buying our capacity or our demonstrated income stream, but rather something that will give you an unfair advantage and thus not something that can easily be quantified." In an unfortunate quirk of language, any purchase that isn't quantifiable by normal valuation standards is considered strategic. The challenge, here, is that the buyer is the party who decides what's strategic—not the seller.

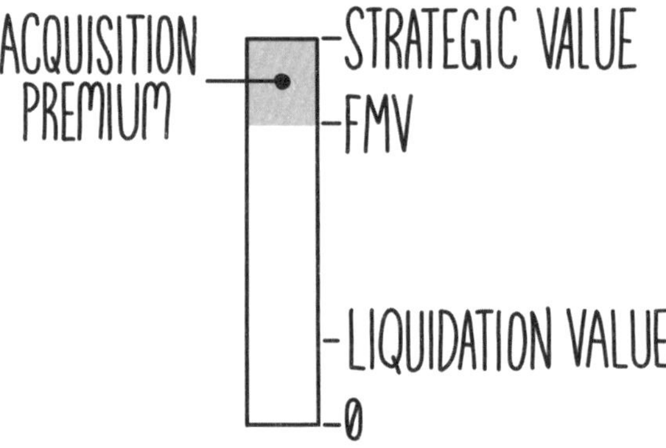

You can sometimes argue that buying your firm will amount to a strategic purchase, and thus not something that can be quantified precisely with a known number (like EBITDA).

What can seal a deal like this, though, is how you, personally, can shift the entire trajectory of the larger firm, which now includes your smaller firm. Maybe you'll build on your existing following, but use your new-found extra time to write a book and bounce around on the speaking circuit for them. Or pinpoint the next few firms that they should purchase to round out this new strategic capability. In these discussions, the reasonable valuation that you secure on your own behalf is just the starting place for negotiations, you don't feel any pressure to accept an offer, and you're in the driver's seat because of what you've built and how unique your firm is in the marketplace. In other words, you aren't just one of 20 firms they might purchase, but rather the one that makes the most sense, and you present the four reasons why that's the case.

So those are the most likely avenues to attack a valuation that you think is too low. Even if you aren't at a point where you need a valuation, it's good to understand these things before you do.

18

TERMS AND OTHER ELEMENTS TO NEGOTIATE

You've seen this phrase a lot, here: "The terms are more important than the price." Let me illustrate the point: You have a great lemonade stand in the neighborhood. Everybody loves you. You rush home from grade school every day and set it up in the shade under the tree closest to the front street, hoping to be all ready when people drive home from work. It's become a neighborhood tradition and your best friend is jealous of your success. You've started whining about how you're bored with it, a little bit, and wish you could play with your friends instead of sitting at the table, even though you have to admit that you're making quite a bit of money—way more than just the allowance you depended on in the past.

So your 9-year old friend senses an entrepreneurial opening and offers to buy it from you. You're not really sure he's serious, but you play along and say, "Sure! Why not! How about $20?"

He swallows hard, realizes that he only has $5, but promises to go back to his parents and see what they think about this idea. Mind you, this friend is a lot of fun to play with, but the kid is really irresponsible. He loses his money, he spends it on crazy things, and he changes his mind a lot, starting all sorts of things but not finishing many of them.

He's gone for a half-hour or so and then comes back with a big smile on his face. "Hey, my parents said I could do it. Here's $5 to get us started. I promise you I'll get the rest. In fact, you can have all the money I make until I pay you off."

Price is important, but there are many other things to negotiate well when you sell your firm.

That's what we would call "$5 cash at closing and a 100% earnout for the remaining 75% of the purchase, contingent on exactly nothing." The kid changes his mind all the time, he's not reliable, and as soon as he sees you playing with all the neighborhood kids, like he's done every day before this acquisition, he's going to miss that and come join you. And you'll have $5 plus maybe a day or two of sales at $.25/glass.

If you really want to sell this thing, and if you're smart, and have no other buyers, you'll get him to borrow the rest of the money ($15) from his parents, and then they'll be left holding the bag.

But if they're onto this kid (their own kid, as it happens) and know that's a bad idea, here's what you'd do instead: "Hey, man. I know you're getting another $5 this Saturday for your allowance. Give me the $5 you have and the $5 you're getting and we'll call it even."

You're done with this thing, anyway, and $10 (a lower price, but paid 100% in cash at closing) is a whole lot more than $5 plus the $15 that never comes.

And then, if you don't have a noncompete with the little sucker, open up another stand, but maybe sell cupcakes or something that you're not yet bored with.

Terms are more important than price. So let's talk about some of the basic terms that you'll need to think carefully about. This is just a primer, so I'll just list the more important ones to consider and how you might think about each one. This will arm you when the time comes, but it also might suggest some different ways that you might handle the discussions with a buyer.

Stock vs. Asset

This is a huge issue, and you really need to consult with someone about it before making any decision. Even if the buyer will have a lot to say about how they want to structure the transaction, you'll need to understand it well because there will be significant implications for you. This will be especially important for cross-border transactions. For example, an acquisition target in Canada will often have significant incentives to structure the purchase of their firm as a stock sale because of how taxes are excluded in certain cases.

What is a stock sale? It means they purchase (usually) all of your shares and everything that comes with that: your assets and obligations and client relationships and goodwill and so on.

What is an asset sale? Usually it's the same thing, but without the stock, and maybe without the balance sheet. In the purchase agreement, you keep the stock but agree to transfer everything that the buyer is purchasing.

Arguments for a Stock Sale

Here's why the buyer or seller or even both might push for a stock sale:

- It's smoother. The buyer doesn't have to set up all new vendor relationships, move employees to a different payroll system, register different corporate officers, and dozens of other things. In other words, it's simple and efficient.
- Client relationships aren't automatically disrupted. Many of the contracts that you might have with large clients will contain "change of control" clauses, which automatically void the relationship. That seldom actually happens, of course, but it's friction in the client relationship and it has to be addressed.
- Any special status that the firm holds may no longer apply. If you are a women-owned or minority-owned business, it's not likely that you're actually landing business because of that designation, but the company hiring your firm gets credit for choosing your firm, and that may no longer apply.
- Taxation can be a big issue, but of course this is very complex. Sometimes sellers want a stock sale precisely because they will be taxed at a lower capital gains rate.
- Depending on your corporate structure and whether or not this is even true, some buyers may want to take advantage of any net operating losses that have been "carried forward," as they say.

Arguments for an Asset Sale

Here's why the buyer or seller or even both might push for an asset sale:

- There's some doubt about the integrity of the financials and there's no time or desire to spend the money to get them audited. This essentially leaves any questions behind, because the buyer knows what they are getting now and not what happened in the past.
- A lawsuit against a corporation, for a wrongful dismissal suit or anything like that, will be inherited by whoever owns the stock now, even if the events occurred before the transaction boundary. The seller can always indemnify the buyer for any such unknown factor, but that indemnification is only as strong as the seller can provide, either personally or via some policy that they have purchased. The entity bringing the action hasn't agreed to that arrangement, and so the buyer needs to know that the seller can withstand that action without it spilling over onto them.
- The same is true of any taxation issue that surfaces after the transaction, but which occurred within that auditable period. Unless it's a huge issue, usually that's 3 years. But say there was an inadvertent tax error made 2 years ago and that doesn't surface until 6 months after the transaction closes. In that case, the buyer is also on the hook, along with the seller, and they are trying to avoid that.
- One of the most complex phrasing you'll find in a final agreement relates to how things will be "trued up" after the transaction. That final adjustment might come from some of the "cash at closing" money that was held in escrow, or it might be deducted from any earnout payments. These are things like a client not paying, a miscalculation in how working capital was determined, how far along

you really were in a "work in progress" calculation, and dozens of other things. To avoid that, sometimes the buyer will just say, in effect, "keep your stock (and maybe give us this in working capital) and you can worry about all that stuff."

- There can be tax benefits to the buyer because of what you'll hear as a "stepped up" basis, leading toward a more favorable depreciation scenario.
- Maybe the buyer doesn't actually want everything you own, and an asset sale makes it easier to pick and choose what they purchase. Maybe you've mistakenly had your operating corporation buy the building where the business is housed (always a bad mistake) and they don't need the building. Or it could relate to IP where they don't agree on the value.
- They may not want to inherit your particular tax structure. Maybe it's a "C" corp from way back and there are not any losses to take advantage of, etc.

This will come up, eventually, and it's in your best interest to get a feel for it sooner rather than later. It's also an area where you absolutely need a good CPA or tax attorney to guide you.

Retained Equity Positions

Say the buyer is only purchasing a portion of your firm. The point of this section is that you need to have some plan for what will happen to the firm next—and I do mean more than just their hopes and dreams about it. This is particularly true if they purchase a majority of your firm, effectively gaining control.

What I mean specifically is that the target should be

defined, the gun loaded, cocked, and aimed. And all that remains is pulling the trigger down the road. When you give a ring to someone and ask them to marry you, you're effectively removing that person from the dating pool. When someone buys 51% of your firm, what are you going to do with the remaining 49% one day? If a price hasn't been established, or at least a formula, as well as the attendant terms for the transaction, you won't be bargaining from a position of strength. There is likely only one buyer—the majority shareholder—and it'll be quite a challenge to get a credible offer from a third party which, if you do, could be matched by the majority owner.

Working Capital Expectations

Working capital is essentially defined as the difference between your short-term assets (AR, cash, etc.) and your short-term liabilities (AP, credit cards, etc.). It's natural for the buyer to not want to start over and have to fund the working capital needs of the newly acquired firm, on top of what they've already paid. And it's natural for the seller to want to keep, at least, all the extra capital that isn't needed to run the firm—and maybe even *all* the working capital if the buyer doesn't need it.

The problem is that this doesn't usually come up until much later, and by that time you're already clinging to some assumptions about how much money you'll get in the sale, and this point will surely disappoint you.

No buyer will come out and give you a definitive answer on the terms of the sale when you are just starting to have these private discussions, but you can ask something like this: "I know that we have a long way to go before we know what this would look like, but how have you handled working capital in the past? Do you assume that some of it will be in included in the sale? We run a very tight ship and keep enough cash in the business to help us navigate ups and downs, and some of it is just extra that we've left there."

Middle Allocations

You don't see this too often, and it's not called a "middle allocation," but it's an interesting way for a buyer to pull off a sale that they otherwise could not, and it's something you should be open to.

I'm referring to a third element of possible terms between the "cash at closing" and "money paid during earnout:" a note, secured or not, that is paid to you.

Imagine a transaction where the buyer and seller are pretty much on the same page regarding the price, and they've begin a discussion of reasonable terms for the payment of that price, but the buyer just doesn't have enough unattached cash—or doesn't want to incur a loan—to pull it off. In that case, you might receive these three things, instead of just the first and the last in this list of three:

- Some percentage of the transaction in cash at closing.
- A seller note.
- A traditional sort of earnout based on whatever you agree to.

That middle option is what we're referring to, here. It's called a seller note because you are a lender. The buyer would use this technique to get money out of the earnout but not have to come up with it in cash at closing.

If you accept something like this, it's very important that it be secured by collateral, and that your options if a default is not remedied give you some power in the transaction (like reversing it). If the buyer is fiscally healthy, then you should back up a step and ask why they need to do it. Make sure that there are no clauses in the agreement that would legitimately allow them to withhold the unpaid portion. But if the buyer is not fiscally healthy—which is probably why they are contemplating this in the first place—you have to decide how much risk you want to take. Obviously, the corporation needs to be on the hook, but you may want to get a personal guarantee, too, even though it can be a bit awkward to ask for it. (That's why you have advisors.) That doesn't mean you'll get paid if everything falls apart, but it means that they'll work a lot harder to get you paid to avoid all that pain and bad publicity coming their way in a bankruptcy.

Expense Assignments

This element will only be included in a discussion of terms if part of your earnout will be calculated based on profitability of some sort, and here's how it usually plays out. You're told that you'll receive the earnout if you meet certain profitability targets. You go back to your spreadsheets and see how often you've hit them and maybe why you missed them in a period or two, calculating whether you can do a better job in the future. You get comfortable with the idea, and the transaction moves forward.

After the celebrations and the ritualistic changing of the LinkedIn profile, you receive a notice from "corporate" about how you narrowly missed the earnout target. "So sad. Please accept our condolences. Try harder next time." But thankfully via a handwritten note, hoping it won't sting as much.

What happened? What happened is that they never told you, or you never asked, about how your profit would be calculated. If you are being swallowed up in a big corporation, where marketing is centralized, for example, you may find an expense allocation on there for a few percentage points. Or a contribution to the expense for the HQ in NYC.

Just make sure you know whether profit will be calculated differently than you have been doing it. The easiest way to accomplish that is to ask their accounting department to recast your last year or so to show you what your profit might have been when accounting for those new allocations.

Financial Guarantees

We talked about how and why you might achieve more certainty about a seller note, but this concern should apply to every financial promise that's made to you. Now, if you're a little fish being swallowed by a big whale, you don't likely need to worry about them scrounging around for quarters under the couch cushions to pay what you're still owed a few years from now (although, come to think of it, Silicon Valley Bank, Lehman Bros, and I rest my case). But what if you have an honest question about the financial health of the buyer?

There's kind of a three-step process that a seller might take, usually through an advisor:

1. Ask a lot of questions about how they operate, what the investing public thinks, scuttlebutt in the news, etc. If you still have questions:
2. Ask for financial statements. They'll certainly object, at which point you say, "well, the alternative is 100% of the purchase price in cash at closing, which I think you said you weren't entertaining, and so I do have a vested interest in knowing about the money that isn't paid at closing." If they object to this (and most won't), then:
3. See if you can settle on a neutral third party that you both agree to, who will evaluate the financial

> stability of this firm and issue a duplicate of the report to each of you. That way they can keep the numbers from you (which might raise a red flag) and you can be assured that all will be fine. This would be an accounting firm, and the buyer would pay for it.

Noncompete & Carveouts

There's more uncertainty around noncompete agreements these days than there has been in the past, but regardless of where all this shakes out, it's easier to enforce a noncompete agreement that a buyer might have with a seller than an employer might have with an employee. For one thing, any agreement the buyer might sign is "in consideration" of something. In other words, they weren't forced to do it, but willingly gave up something (their employment options) to get something else (money).

The buyer, too, would have a reasonable interest in your continued role in the combined entity. If they didn't think highly of you and your work, they wouldn't be thinking about giving you a lot of money. And yes, the earnout kind of guarantees that the seller will stick around and put a shoulder to the plow, but what if there's a change of heart?

In that case, the seller can just walk away and leave the rest of the money on the table (the seller couldn't be forced to stick around, ever since we fixed the Constitution and passed the all-important law in 1865), and the buyer would just have to live with that. The noncompete is meant as a safety net to keep the seller from creating some competitive entity that would undermine the purchase in the first place.

To operate within a modern legal environment, the agreement might say, "okay, you can take clients, but you have to pay us some (crazy high) percentage of all your billings from those clients." Either way, you'll have a strong incentive to not start something—or even go work somewhere—that might be frowned on by the buyer. And remember, even if you're right, they have a lot more money than you do, and probably more time, to fight this out.

That's reasonable, I think, but what if the buyer defaults after the transaction closes? In other words, they miss a structured payment or they don't remit some earnout amount on time or in full? This is one of the most glaring omissions in M&A work, and it's one that we will always fight for:

1. Buyer defaults on something.
2. Buyer doesn't cure that default within the defined time period.
3. Seller is released from noncompete and keeps all the money they've been paid.

That third point is the one to fight for. Now, if the buyer goes bankrupt or closes, that might very well make the noncompete null and void, but that's not usually what happens.

If your buyer can't meet their obligations to you, and after you've patiently given them some time to fix it, you should be able to keep all the money you've already received, take any clients you brought, and do whatever you want.

Finally, you want to make sure that the noncompete has a carveout for anything you might do, at least that you know about now. Maybe you want to sit on a board or do pro bono work for a cherished nonprofit. The buyer needs to know about this and approve, of course, but also make sure that the employment agreement that will accompany the purchase agreement explicitly allows for it.

Employment Agreement

On the other side of a noncompete is an employment agreement. After all, if they fire you, for cause or just because they don't like how you dress, it's going to be quite difficult to capture whatever portion of your earnout remains.

Some purchase agreements aren't tied to your ongoing employment at the firm, but if they are, then you need to have a matching employment agreement. Unless you do something really heinous, you should have the right to stick around and earn that money, and we haven't even mentioned all the lost wages you're forfeiting if you aren't there.

They will still be able to fire you, but it should be very difficult to do. And you'll probably deserve it.

Assumption of Financial Obligations

Obligations usually fall into three big categories:

- **Unsecured.** The cleaning company bill you get for your triple-net leased facility would fall into this category. If you don't pay it, it's probably not worth taking you to court over it, either, and if they do win a judgment, it'll be even more difficult to collect.
- **Secured.** These are the obligations where they can "repossess" something from you to settle things up. Think of it like a pawn shop. "Okay, I'll give you $100, but I'm going to keep your guitar. You can buy it back or not, but I want something for something." In the big financial world, you would secure something with corporate assets, like securing your credit line with your accounts receivable, or you might secure it with personal assets, like an installment loan for your business that is secured by

your home. Eventually, the bank is going to take your home and sell it to make themselves whole.

- **Not immune to bankruptcy.** People usually forget about this one, but I'm including it here just to be complete. In this category are taxes and student loans, with some exceptions.

In this section on the terms that you'll need to negotiate, there won't be any dispute about which obligations the buyer has to take over. There might be disagreement, but not dispute. After you both settle on the purchase agreement, driven largely by whether it's a stock or asset sale, you shouldn't see any surprises.

But hidden inside some of those obligations is your own personal guarantee, and there's no reason you should ever personally guarantee something after a transaction closes. This usually applies to credit cards, by default, and a credit line. But look through all of your operating leases, capital leases, and banking relationships to make sure.

This is usually handled by paying down the credit line and closing it. The same thing with the credit cards: Pay them off and let the buyer open new ones.

Leasing an Owned Facility

This has happened a fair bit, honestly, and it's important to get some idea in your head about how you're going to handle it.

Your business—the one that you are selling—might lease a facility that you own, personally, usually in a separate corporation. By the way, you always want that in a separate corporation, for three reasons:

1. There are tax advantages.

2. It isn't subject to a judgment that's granted against your company.
3. Any buyer you have might not want the building.

It's this third reason we're addressing, here, and the first thing you do is to acknowledge the interests that each party has. You, the seller want to continue that stream of cash from the business that's renting your building, or at least you want time to make other arrangements by selling the building or finding another tenant. And the buyer wants flexibility. They may already have a workplace in town that has extra space, or they intend for everyone to go remote, or they think they can find a cheaper facility to lease (or buy).

The way to resolve this is often a reasonable compromise. The buyer agrees to a new lease, at market rent, for a short period of time (a year or two), with an option to renew. That gives both parties the flexibility they need.

So all of these elements, and more, need to be negotiated. How many things should be settled in the LOI that you receive, or is it okay to figure out a lot of them later during and after their due diligence phase? That's what we'll tackle next.

19

PRELOADING THE LOI

If a buyer is serious, you're eventually going to get an LOI (letter of intent). This is a written document that doesn't really promise anything, but it does specify their intent. Think of an LOI like this:

We don't yet know enough about your firm, but we've learned enough about it that our intent is to go through with this purchase. We're proposing that we purchase your firm for [price], and we'll pay you [cash at closing] and the rest of the purchase price will be paid to you like this: [earnout]. We reserve the right to change the price or the terms, but we're serious enough that we'd like to verify our assumptions and then formalize later. You in?

Think of it as dating you, and thus taking you off the marriage market. It's not a proud dating where they want everyone to know (yet), and they might be dating other people, too, but this is a serious signal that something might happen.

The only way you know it's serious, by the way, is that they are fixin' to spend a whole bunch of time and money verifying the assumptions that they've made. There will be advisors, attorneys, and accountants. Of course, you'll be spending money on the same things, too, which is why you have to decide how serious you are, as well.

In this process, you need to understand the philosophical approach of the buyer—and there are really two kinds of buyers. On the one hand, you have the serious, respectful suitor who has had many conversations with you and already figured out what this might look like, what your strengths and weaknesses are, who they might want to keep in the transaction, and dozens of other things. They wrap all this up in an LOI and the process from here on out is just to make sure they haven't missed anything. The time period before the LOI is longer and the time period after it is shorter.

How much detail you should insist on when signing an LOI is a philosophical decision that impacts the process.

Then there are the buyers who are dating around like a speed dating show on reality TV. They find multiple firms that might meet their specifications, if they even have them, and they throw LOIs at a bunch of them. After you sign one, they'll learn what they should have learned in the first place. They might pursue a sale with one of them and leave the rest at the altar. “So sorry.” These are the buyers with very short time intervals before the LOI and very long intervals afterward.

When you get a loose LOI from someone who clearly doesn’t understand you enough to make a detailed, meaningful offer, chances are good that they are scattering LOIs everywhere and intending to negotiate later. This is bad because:

- They are dating multiple people and you really have no idea how badly they want you.
- It’s going to tie you up with busy work—which they often delegate downward—as they clarify some of the things that they should have understood in the first place.
- That LOI will often come with a no-shop clause, and you’ll effectively be off the market. “Hey, I’ve invited eight girls to the dance. I’ll let one of you know who’s really going later, but for now, you can’t entertain any other offers.”
- They’ll use the “sunk cost” thing against you. In other words, you’ve invested all this effort after the LOI. Do you really want to walk away from all that and start over with someone else?

We strongly prefer to negotiate as much as we can into an LOI, and then view the due diligence period as having two purposes:

- To verify the assumptions the buyer made in crafting the offer and to surface any mistakes that either party made.
- To dig deeper into the specifics of important issues, like how we’ll calculate the transfer of working capital and so on.

This "speed dating" concept is a key philosophical approach to buying and selling firms. Not only does it impact all the time and energy you might have to put into their many requests on the way to getting to know each other, but you are effectively off the market during that entire period, regardless of what you or they discover along the way. You may quickly find that your cultures are not at all compatible and notify them that the transaction is off—but you're still going to be bound by the no-shop clause.

A no-shop clause is essentially an agreement you make to not try to sell your firm to someone else. It'll state that you can't have any discussions, substantive or not, with any other buyer during that period, which will typically be between 3 and 6 months. And if any potential buyer reaches out to you during that period, you have to report that to the buyer whose no-shop clause you signed, giving them an unfair advantage in negotiations. This no-shop clause will bind your advisors, too. They can't act like NFL agents who regularly "tamper" with contracts during the period when it's not allowed.

Yes, you'll spend time (and money) kind of the same way, regardless of whether it's before or after the LOI is signed. Just know that after you've inked the LOI you'll be locked into the courtship, while they're free to keep seeing other people as you whisper through your tears, "please choose me!"

If you do sign a no-shop clause prematurely and quickly find that you don't want to sell your firm to these people, you can just tell them that and ask them to release you from the no-shop clause. But usually you'll just have to wait it out and spin the search up again after the clause expires.

If there is a no-shop clause, it'll be incorporated in the LOI, and you'll want to look at those terms carefully. The language will also offer cues about the buyer's intention. The more specific the LOI, the more serious the buyer, and the more likely the transaction is to be consummated.

What happens after you sign an LOI? That's the period during which the buyer conducts a due-diligence process to verify any assumptions in the LOI. We'll cover that in a later chapter, but first let's talk about an earnout.

20

CRAFTING A REASONABLE EARNOUT

Think of an earnout as the conditions under which you'll get all the rest of the money that is not paid to you in cash at closing. In some transactions, the purchase price is paid entirely at closing; in other words, there are no conditions that will or will not be met later after the firm is sold.

Getting paid in full when all the papers are signed is quite rare, but it happens, and the triggers for it make sense. Maybe it'll be very difficult to track the performance of your firm afterward because you'll quickly be integrated into the buyer's firm. Or maybe you're being purchased by one of your own clients, and they expect your other clients to abandon you, slowly, over time, and don't really expect you to recruit new clients that will in effect be competitors to the acquirer. We even did a transaction, once, where the seller was being appointed to a high government office, the terms of which didn't allow any conflict of interest involving an ownership position in a business that might involve the government, and so there could be no earnout because his actions might influence the outcome, one way or another. And finally, you'll sometimes see that the seller is moving on, by choice or because of some health issue.

But for most transactions, most of the price is divided into some amount of cash at closing and the remainder during an earnout.

For the record, the earnout is a fairly modern concept that's now widespread. Earnouts first appeared in the 1980s, and were then widely used in the 1990s and beyond. Their rise reflected the use of acquisitions as a business tool, and the fact that those acquisitions carried more and more risk for the buyer. They allowed the buyer to pay higher prices to the seller, but still shift some of that risk to what actually happened after the transaction closed.

The terms of the earnout describe the obstacles you'll have to navigate to actually maximize the sale.

With that wider use of earnouts came more scrutiny from accounting bodies, which wanted to ensure that buyers were properly disclosing everything they were on the hook for after the transaction. This helped make earnouts more transparent and, hopefully, predictable. Then, as you would expect, earnouts were challenged in court, putting more pressure on how they were spelled out and calculated. There is typically a direct relationship between an earnout's structure and the uncertainty that a buyer has about what'll happen after the transaction closes.

Elements of an Earnout

An earnout will address these things:

- The formula for calculating the payment(s).
- The time periods for that calculation.
- Any dependencies.

The formula is mutually agreed upon, but the earnout is an offer from the buyer and will reflect what's most important to them. Everything they pay to you in cash at closing is gone, forever, and the earnout is both a mechanism to derisk the remaining portion of the purchase and a very specific incentive for the behavior they want from you.

(This isn't entirely true in that some of the cash paid at closing might be deposited into an escrow account, which is trued up later, but that's really just an administrative thing to make the demands of due diligence less onerous.)

The recent trend in earnouts has been to simplify them and tie them to the most important thing the buyer wants, like continued growth, profitability, or something else. But in rare cases you will still see complex earnouts.

The unit of time is almost always a year, and the number of units is almost always 1, 2, or 3 years. Five years was standard in the past, but you'll hardly ever find an earnout that lasts that long. The world is changing too fast.

The dependencies are simple requirements that will trigger an actual payment for meeting the earnout's goals. This might be something like your continued presence, not being charged with a felony, adherence to a noncompete, etc.

Let's go into this in more detail.

Understand the Incentives

"Show me the incentives and I'll show you the outcome," Charlie Munger famously said. While it's certainly fair for the buyer to load up an earnout with incentives to achieve certain goals together, there's also a diminishing return in relying too much on them. Here's how a conversation might unfold.

Buyer: *We're excited about buying your firm. Our main, and almost singular, purpose is to help build our HR consulting practice. It's not something we do now, and we think there's a lot of opportunity there. We're beyond excited.*

Seller: *That's great. I see that you've built up a change management practice, too. How's that going? And do you see any cross-selling opportunities between the two if we make this work?*

Buyer: *Great question. It's going well, but maybe not as well as we had hoped. There's a bit of room for improvement. We had some management changes along the way and lost a bit of momentum. Actually, they could probably learn a lot from you and how your team has maintained a really consistent growth trajectory.*

Seller: *Uhm. Yeah, I can see that. But let me ask a question. The earnout that you are proposing is tied exclusively to how my new department is performing, which is why you want to keep separate books so that both of us can track how well we do after we're brought into the mothership. I can see how it'll be natural—and probably a good idea—for me to be involved in guiding the change management group, cross-selling their services, helping them close big deals for that department, and so on. I'm a team player, for sure, but I'm worried that I'm kinda not going to have the financial incentive to do anything but focus on my own department. Any way we could address this?*

And then the conversation starts, because the incentives are pretty much going to guarantee the outcome. Maybe the incentive is tied instead to the overall growth of the company and not just your department, in which case you'll have your own questions about how much is in your control or not. Or maybe it's split. Or maybe it's removed entirely. Incentives can be a good thing, but they can really be bad, too.

When I think of incentives, I think of that time in a science lab in high school when the teacher paired me with great students or loser students. Under my breath, I was saying, "Geez. I ought to just let these other three fellow students gossip while I do the real work." Or, "This is fantastic. We can divide and conquer and crush the other teams with our collective strength."

There's a psychological element to this, too. The more complex the incentive arrangements, the less motivating they are. If I want Frida, our 160-lb Great Dane, to bring the ball back and drop it at my feet, I'll give her a treat to do it. I'm not going to tell her she has to do that within 2.5 seconds or she doesn't get a treat. No, drop the ball and get a treat. (Hit this simple target and get the earnout.) For the record, she never drops the ball, so this is purely a hypothetical. And while I know a lot about incentives in earnouts, I clearly know nothing about how to construct earnouts with dogs.

Careful What You Promise

It's pretty easy to make promises meant to put the buyer's mind at ease about something, but it's really, really important to remember how quickly these can bite you in the butt.

Imagine a conversation unfolding like this:

Buyer: *Hey, your most recent full year was actually really good. Strong growth from the previous year and you added eight percentage points to your EBITDA. That's the kind of performance we're looking for, and we want to make sure it's not an aberration from the previous two years, which were kind of flat. What's your thinking on that?*

Seller: *Fair point. We were initially worried about the same thing, but here's why that was not a one-time thing but actually the new normal. [Blah, blah, blah ... lots of BS promises and hype.]*

Buyer: *Ah! I see now what you mean. [Gives understanding look to their partner, sitting across the table.] Let's do this, then. How about we build that assumption into the earnout. You seem confident that you'll maintain this level of performance and we're very happy to reward it.*

Boom. You just got took, as they say, because now they'll make you eat your words. The buyer rightfully expects you to make projections, but don't make projections that are so damning that they make you eat them in an earnout. Don't write checks in your early discussions that you can't cash in an earnout.

What Earnouts Are Tied To

As you would expect, earnouts can be tied to anything that's important to the buyer. In an ideal world, the earnout is tied to the purpose of the acquisition, and it's pegged to that simple metric. Say the acquisition is being tied to added EBITDA, which is darn easy to measure, so tie the earnout to that but don't let them tell you how to achieve it.

You'll find earnouts most commonly linked to these things:

- Top-line revenue targets.
- Profitability targets, either measured by net revenue (before EBITDA allowances are made) or just purely EBITDA targets.
- Growth trajectories, like maintaining a 20% YoY target.
- Retention of a particular client, especially if your revenue has come in part from a client concentration risk (i.e., one related source of revenue

is a higher percentage than the buyer is comfortable with).
- Milestones that might deliver continued success: regulatory approval, rolling out a product or service on time, etc.

This is where you might want to retroactively model this out, either using your own team to do it or the buyer's financial people. This will help you see what would have happened if, say, events had unfolded differently in the past. It will also confirm how the buyer is going to calculate it, which is an argument for having them do that for you.

Cliffs vs. Graduated Targets

The LOI, or the later purchase agreement, might arrive on your desk with cliffs for hitting performance targets. "Achieve a net profit of 18% and you'll get an additional $160,000 payment at the close of the annual reporting period, no later than 60 days following that close."

When you read that, your first thought should be: What happens if I hit 17%? And thus will begin the very necessary negotiation to replace those cliff targets with graduated or sloped targets. The ideal adjustment would be something like this: The 18% target will be paid proportionally. In other words, achieving a 9% net profit will result in receiving one-half of the $160,000, or $80,000.

That's probably not what's going to happen, but you absolutely must protect yourself in the event that you get close to the target but don't actually hit it, ensuring that you get something and not nothing.

Failing some reasonable resolution, your last best option is to retain the right to make up that goal deficiency in the next period. Say you miss it in the first period, by just a little bit, but blow the goal out of the water in the second period. Maybe any excess performance they aren't going to give you credit for could be applied retroactively.

In that same vein, you want to be careful about maximum ceilings. Say you negotiate a sloped sort of arrangement like I've just suggested, and you're eligible to earn more than the $160,000 (using the same illustration) if you achieve a net profit greater than 18%. If the negotiations start to get weird—because there definitely is a diminishing return in arguing about everything—just explain that you just don't want any incentives to manipulate when revenue hits the books, which is exactly what's going to happen if they get too cute in the targets you need to meet. More on that later.

How Your Employment Agreement Fits

In simple terms, you need an employment agreement, and it needs to match the length of the earnout. This fact will give you one piece of ammunition, among others, in negotiating a shorter earnout, because they'll be stuck paying you during the entire term of the earnout and they may want more flexibility than that.

Here's why that's important. Picture a transaction where 70% of the purchase price is paid in cash at closing, with a 2-year earnout during which, if you hit reasonable targets, you'll be paid another 15% at the close of each year.

But your boss leaves after 9 months, or they acquire another company, or there's some big downturn, or they just don't like you, and for whatever reason they fire you, and the "cause" (or "reason") isn't something you agree with.

When that happens, not only will you lose your salary and benefits (and possibly your dignity), but you'll be untethered from this company, and you'll have zero influence on whether or not the department—your former company—left behind can perform in such a way that the earnout is achieved. You're sitting over here watching your kid driving the car and who knows what they'll hit. Scream all you want, but you're powerless.

That's why a matching employment agreement makes sense. It not only protects your earnout, but also your compensation, your title, and your responsibilities. In a good setting where there's reasonable people all around, you'll work with them if those things need to change, but you need some legal leverage, which you might willingly give up, later, if it's truly in your best interest to do so. You absolutely need to work with an attorney on this. An advisor might be able to outline the basic tenets, but this requires an attorney's mind to shape it in a way that's enforceable in whatever jurisdiction is chosen for disputes (these things vary a lot by state).

One last thought: You may not think too much about this, now, but keep in mind that you may very well need some carveouts to whatever noncompete is sandwiched with the employment agreement, and these fall into two categories:

- The things you are already doing or intend to do that don't strike you as a competitive activity, but which you want to clear with the buyer. These might include serving on a board, donating your expertise to a nonprofit, etc. Just raise them and get their approval, preferably in writing.
- The things you will want to do if/when you leave employment, regardless of the circumstances (for cause or otherwise). Say you have a noncompete that prevents you from starting another competitive firm, owning part of a competitive firm, or even working at one. Maybe you feel like you have to agree to this in order to drag the purchase across the finish line. Here the obvious carveout is to be able to

> accept a job on the client side rather than the firm you are working for, now. Maybe it's not for a client currently being served by the buyer, but you need to give yourself options, even if you aren't sure you'll need them.

One of those options deserves its own section, and that's to be prepared for the very rare case where something goes terribly wrong. That's next.

The Big Reversal

Every purchase agreement (that's the last thing you sign, after the LOI and due diligence and any final adjustments) will spell out what happens if either party doesn't meet their obligations.

For example, let's say the buyer defaults by not remitting an earnout payment to you. They have a certain number of days to do it and they miss the target. You can bend with them (at your own peril), or you can perk up and pay attention. You'll typically have to give them written notice that they've defaulted (not met their promises), and the buyer will have the opportunity, then, to cure that default (keep their promise, retroactively, maybe with a penalty) within a certain period of time.

But what happens if they don't? If a buyer misses some major milestone—and this is especially true if there's a significant penalty attached to that—something is probably seriously wrong, and here's where you need to protect yourself.

Here's our standard suggestion when negotiating purchase agreements: You keep everything you have received and are released from any noncompete. You're still going to lose, because you have to start over. But at least you're free to do what you want, including taking any legacy clients with you, and you don't have to sell the boat you bought with the money you collected at closing and repay it to them. (I guess you could just park the boat in their front lawn, but doing that late at night carries its own risks.)

Summary

When you analyze the earnout, here are the things to look at:

- Does it incentivize the right things?
- Will it be easy to calculate?
- What will happen if I don't hit the desired target?
- Am I going to be carrying the same risk?

This last point is probably the most important one in the entire chapter. If the earnout means that you'll retain nearly all the entrepreneurial risk you have now—but with a boss who will have a fair bit of control over your activities—why not just go it alone and keep all of the upside rather than carrying on the good fight for someone else and keeping just some of it?

One of the main reasons you started and are running your firm is that you're basically unemployable, except for this brief period of time otherwise known as an earnout. So if you're going to subject yourself to having a boss again, by all the good things that grow on God's green earth, you'd better be compensated for stepping back into an employment situation again, and that's what an earnout is.

Please think about this very carefully. The earnout is where the tradeoffs lie, and you must understand them. Speaking of understanding things, let's talk about your leverage.

21

UNDERSTANDING YOUR LEVERAGE

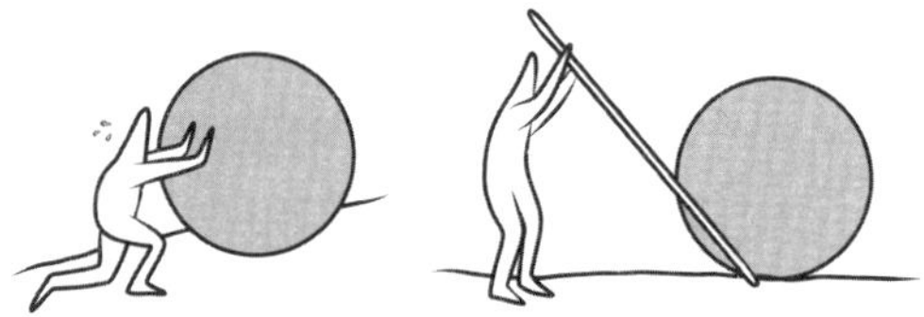

Your leverage in negotiating a transaction boils down to the things we worked through in Chapter 7 "Reasons a Buyer Might Want Your Firm," but exercising that leverage is a different thing. It starts with knowing *what* a buyer cares about, and even more so, *how much* they care about those things—but that has to be played against *what* you care about, and *how much* you care about those things.

It's important to distinguish between the real reason a buyer might want your firm and their negotiables because they can differ. For example, maybe they really need a unique capability that your firm offers. They want to bolt it onto their offerings because the marketplace wants to buy those things together. Over and over their clients have asked for that offering and they have to go somewhere else to get it, and the possible buyer of your firm doesn't want their clients to be with anyone else at the high school dance.

They have two choices at that point: build it, slowly, and without many clients who are already buying it, or buy it, more quickly, in a transaction that brings clients with it. On top of that, they'll get to sell what they already do into the clients that accompany the transaction.

They explain all this in the early stages, and it seems like a great fit to both parties, but then the ugliness of negotiation shines the cold light of day onto your financials and they use those against you. Their profitability is 29% and you've struggled to hit 8%. Everybody knows that they aren't buying you for your profit, since they primarily want your capability, but they reallocate the value of the transaction around profit instead of the capability. That's just one of the games you'll encounter in the back and forth.

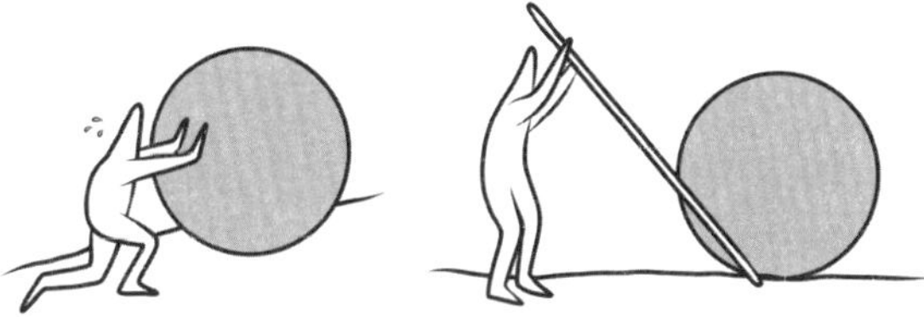

Understanding your leverage in the transaction will guide your negotiation strategy.

All of those things are part of the long dance of negotiation, and your mental approach to this is important. Don't take any of it personally. If you're pretty good at compartmentalizing these shenanigans and just smiling (while you're fuming inside), it could be a deeper cultural problem that's sending you a bigger message: Do you want to be in bed with these people?

But if the cultural fit is there, just think of the negotiation as a fun challenge. Play the long game, don't lose sight of the bigger picture, and just be better at negotiation than they are. This isn't a book about negotiation, so I'll let you find those principles elsewhere, but there are some important things to keep in mind as this unfolds. Six of them, actually. These are the strategies that keep you in the driver's seat as you negotiate your fate ... or future.

Other Suitors

When there's only one firm (at the moment) who's showing interest in buying you, it's a little bit like being an auctioneer when only one bidder shows up. Unless they are really stupid, they aren't going to bid themselves up. We went to a real estate auction for some property that was up for sale next to our farm, recently, and we decided that we were willing to spend $20,000/acre for the plot next to ours. When we showed up, 30 minutes early, the crowd was already gathering and there were probably 150 people there, and 40 of them had registered to participate in the bidding. Another piece of property went first and it sold for $41,000/acre.

Ouch, we're thinking. This cannot be a good sign. It hit us that we'd have to stick to our preset limit or we'd be screwed. In the end, the plot we wanted went for $42,500/acre and we never raised our card and placed a bid. The seller, a nice freshly widowed lady in our neighborhood, had worked with a great auction company that had drummed up all sorts of interest. All the bidders were competing with each other.

There are times when a client comes to us with an interested buyer in hand, and our job is first to maximize the price and minimize the risk for them. And if the transaction still doesn't meet their expectations, we might very well take them to market and find other buyers. This happened one time with a firm in Texas who had an offer in hand from an out-of-state buyer. They asked us to look at it and give them an opinion on whether they should take it.

We immediately thought it was too low, and since they were not yet under a no-shop clause, we suggested that we shop them around. We found five mildly interested parties and received two written offers. We went back to the original would-be buyer and explained our dilemma: They seemed like a great fit for the buyer, but the price was too low. In the end, they raised their offer by 85% and the original transaction went through, but at a better price. Sometimes you use other offers as leverage and sometimes you actually take one of those offers. (An advisor doesn't want to get the reputation of playing games, so they have to legitimately be willing to entertain another offer and not just use it as leverage.)

Try to get more than one bidder at your auction. The first offer you get may come to you organically, but you'll probably need to engage a search firm to find others, and this is where you'd want to be careful about any no-shop clause until you really think this is the one for you.

Negotiating a Complete LOI

You might think that your leverage is linear. Maybe it's greatest at the beginning and then declines over time. That can be true, especially when the weariness of deal negotiation sets in. But it's also true that the buyer's (and seller's!) sunk costs can play a role. "Do we really want to walk away from this after spending all this time and money? Let's just give on this point and make it happen."

Generally, you really want to negotiate all the big things before the LOI (see Chapter 19 "Preloading the LOI," which deals with it in great depth). Think of the due-diligence period as merely confirming all the assumptions and eliminating surprises. On the other hand, the due-diligence period, after the LOI and before the transaction closes, really places the burden on the buyer. They are the ones who may surface additional negotiating points that'll be used against you.

So as much as possible, you want to identify all the salient points ahead of time, build them into the buyer's assumptions as expressed in the LOI, and deny them any ammunition they might find to squeeze you later. Not only that, but it'll build trust in the future relationship because they'll begin to appreciate your transparency in this, and assume it in future dealings.

And most important? You can still be searching for other buyers since you haven't signed the no-shop clause, yet, and so your leverage lasts longer as you negotiate a strong LOI.

Keep a Strong Business

As we also discussed in an earlier chapter, the biggest danger you'll encounter *before* the deal closes—there are many dangers *after* it closes—is neglecting your core business because you assume that this sale will go forward and because you have to spend time on this process and your energy has to come from somewhere.

This benign neglect can also drag you toward a deal when you'd be better off maintaining your independence. There's a good chance that this transaction, and the reason you're considering it in the first place, will address some big challenge that you've been having. Maybe it's new business. So your new business plan is on shaky ground as it is, but if you abandon it even further during the negotiations, it's going to be even harder to pull out and go it alone again. You've lost time, you're even less engaged, and things are a bit bleak.

When you're working through a deal, be hopeful that it'll happen but assume, for business planning purposes, that it won't. Focus on new business, finish building out that service offering, don't abandon all hiring, etc. This will put you in a stronger negotiating position because you aren't afraid to walk away.

Keep the Circle Small

There's a time and a place to bring others into your confidence about what's happening, and we covered that in Chapter 12: "When to Bring Others into the Loop."

But there's one rule of thumb that sellers tend to overlook: Only include certain people at certain points if they'll be fine should the transaction not move forward.

One of the biggest allures for the team in a transaction is the excitement of new things, maybe better benefits or a career ladder with more rungs on it. Once you plant that seed, it will be harder for you to back away from a deal because of the disappointment that it might cause. It shouldn't affect your thinking, but it will.

Biggest Lever of All

In sum, and as a banner over all these reasons, is one massive thing on your part: a willingness to walk away. If you aren't willing to walk away, you'll negotiate differently and the buyer —or the buyer's advisors—will smell the desperation and paint you into many little corners.

You always have to pick your battles, of course, but if this deal must happen, in your mind, you're already at a massive disadvantage.

And if you do walk away, do it gracefully and with transparency and regret. Don't burn any bridges. After all, an opportunity might surface again, and even if it doesn't, the M&A world is a small one and you want the right reputation as someone who negotiates seriously and transparently, and doesn't waste a buyer's time and money.

There are also situations where you might be too willing to walk away, likely because you're *just done* and can't imagine working for someone else again. It's true that the longer you work for yourself the less employable you are, but maybe you need to grind it out for a year for the sake of your team, if for no one else.

We were working for a firm in California, one time. It was a small firm and the transaction was provisionally worth $1.9m, with $1m of that paid in cash at closing. The earnout was dependent on the seller working at the firm, with no need to hit certain performance targets, but he just couldn't. I was about to board my flight to LAX for the closing when the seller texted me and said that he couldn't go through with it. He could have kept the $1m and never stepped foot in the buyer's office again, but there were some mental health issues that left him feeling trapped. His leverage—a willingness to walk away—was understandable, but you need to have a balance if you're doing what's best for your firm, and especially the people who work for you. That means an excitement and a hopefulness about the deal happening, but a willingness to walk away if that's in your best interest. I still wonder if he made the right choice.

By the way, if there's any phase of the process where you're most likely to walk away, it'll definitely be during the due diligence part of it. Let's talk about how to keep it from being a grind. Because you are going to kind of hate it.

22

DUE DILIGENCE

Due diligence is—well, what can I say?—not fun. It's when the buyer brings in their team of experts to verify all the assumptions built into the LOI, and these people are paid to essentially justify their existence. They rub their hands together with glee and laugh under their breath with mirth when they find something that somebody missed. "See, this is why you pay us the big bucks!"

Not really. But kind of.

The best style of due diligence is built on top of a thorough LOI, and so they are verifying very specific things. This is the process you're hoping for. The other type of due diligence is designed to beat you down in a revised LOI, which will leave you standing at a distance and hoping they don't find that the transmission in the car you're selling is leaking oil badly.

The buyer will have carefully vetted the more intangible aspects of your business, like your culture, management style, new business approach, client arrangements, management structure, and so on. Due diligence is more of a nitty-gritty process, and the people leading it will ask for your contracts, your detailed financials, your tax returns, and anything else they want from you, and you'll have to supply it. That could include personal tax returns, too. Essentially they're looking for any mismatches between what you say the company paid you (you're going to fight for a lot) and what you reported to the tax authorities (your incentive is to minimize it).

The due diligence phase is essentially a second round of negotiation where good buyers look to see if their assumptions were correct while bad buyers look for things that they can use against you to tip the transaction in their favor.

There will be a master list request, and your people will drop all the materials into a secure digital "data room" that only certain people will have access to. Then they'll ask for more clarification, which will need to be digital, too, and will be added to that room.

After everybody is satisfied, the attorneys (always on the buyer side) will begin preparing the purchase agreement, which is what you'll sign at closing. Your advisors will need to go through that, carefully, to make sure that it represents everything that's been agreed to. While your M&A advisor will be involved, your attorney will take the lead, and they are the only party really qualified to do that.

The process of due diligence is simpler in an asset sale and more complicated in a stock sale because of the potential liabilities the buyer is guarding against in the latter, like any legal action brought against you or any tax liability that hasn't surfaced yet. Even if they can't find anything, you still might need to indemnify the buyer, and if the transaction is large enough, there might be a third party that insures the buyer from such a hazard.

If the buyer and seller are both in a hurry, and if the dollars aren't all that large, a buyer might breeze through this process, just as you might buy a home "as is" and deal with what you find later. But that's rare and you need to be prepared for a typical due diligence process.

One of the more controversial requests you might get is to let someone from the buyer's team—usually high up on the ladder—meet with your clients. They'll want to see for themselves if the relationship is strong and maybe even get some indication of the client's future plans with your firm. If the buyer insists on this as part of due diligence, you can't really decline their request, but you need to allow it very late in the process. Right near the end, after you've told the client about this possibility. If it happens, it'll likely only happen with your largest clients, and the buyer will usually let that sample speak for the rest.

So when do you have to make a final decision? That's what we'll talk about next.

23

D-DAY: IT'S TIME FOR A DECISION

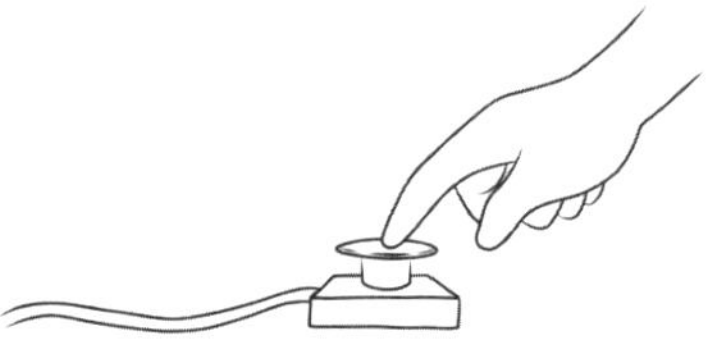

There isn't really one big decision day, but more a series of "yes" markers that build into a signing day. You haven't committed to anything final until you sign the papers at closing, but that's not how you should think.

All the time and money you've spent leading up to the closing is a sunk cost, and you don't want to throw all that away by suddenly changing your mind unless there's a really good reason. So think of the entire process as a series of green lights. You keep driving through them until you see a red one. And the earlier you see a red light, the sooner you can bail and quit wasting time and money (yours and theirs).

But eventually you're going to need to make a firm yes or no decision, and that involves a lot of careful consideration on your part. It starts with the reason you're contemplating a sale in the first place. Will this transaction help you meet that stated goal? Are you okay with losing a fair bit of control over your immediate future?

Several things can drag you forward, almost against your will:

- You've incurred sunk costs (time and money), but the distraction is actually more impactful than the money.
- You've told some people about this already you'd be embarrassed if you had to reverse course.
- You've allowed yourself to dream about that next stage in a way you've never done before, and you can't bear the thought of abandoning that dream.

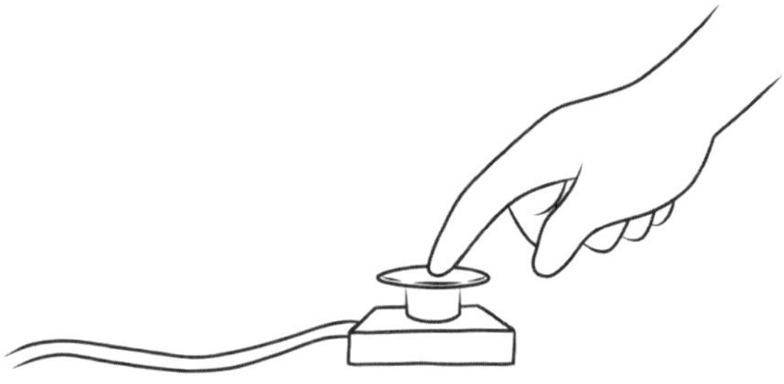

After negotiating through all of the details, in the end you'll have to say "yes" or "no" to this opportunity.

One of the things that an advisor can help you with is called a "crossover analysis." You'll make some assumptions around what an earnout will look like, and then how much money you'll end up with, after taxes, from the cash at closing and the earnouts over time. That's compared with a similar projection of what will happen if you just stay the course and keep getting distributions. Your salary is probably going to be similar in either scenario, so that's not usually a part of the comparison.

The crossover analysis will answer this question: How long do I need to keep running my firm to match the predicted money I'll get in this transaction? (That, of course, only answers the financial question because if you just stay the course, you won't have a boss like you will if you sell the firm.)

The other thing it doesn't account for is this: At the end of the period covered by the crossover analysis, you'd still own a firm. That's good (you can still sell it) and bad (you'll still have to sell it, or just walk away, or merge or acquihire it).

But here's what that exercise points to: Unless you're significantly derisking your current situation, why the heck would you sell your firm?

For example, if the buyer is still requiring you to shoulder all the entrepreneurial risk because you'll need to hit your earnout target in order to make the sale sensible financially, why the heck wouldn't you just keep being an entrepreneur and keep it *all* for yourself—and without a boss?

The big dilemma is always: If I'm going to have a boss during this earnout, maybe that boss ought to be me. In other words, I'm aiming to derisk my situation, but if I'm still shouldering most of the entrepreneurial risk, I might as well retain most of the upside and not give it to them.

But like most all of the big decisions you've made as you've built a valuable firm in the first place, in the end it'll be a gut decision—based on data, yes, but still relying on your instincts. That's fine. You can sell and move on to your next career. Don't worry too much about it, unless you're past retirement age and should have done this many years ago and there's no next after this earnout concludes.

So let's assume you move forward. Now what? But before we cover your new role, let's take a quick look in the next chapter at flipping this whole process and maybe buying a firm. If that's not why you're reading this, and you intend to be the seller in every case, just skip the next chapter.

24

FLIPPING THE PROCESS: BUYING A FIRM

We ought to start by noting that growth shouldn't be a bedrock of your strategy. You aren't likely aiming for a network effect on top of a solid product-market fit, and you can have a wonderful, solid business by just running it well and maximizing for a size that fits your own desired mix of "doing the work" and "managing the people who do the work." Some of the bigger firms out there don't take as much money home for the principals as some of the smaller firms. It's all a choice ... as long as you're in charge and the business isn't dragging you around, it's all good.

You might have been thinking of yourself as a seller, all along, but then when reading this book you realize that you don't have quite enough to sell and get rich on, and so you think maybe you should pause your plans and build a bigger firm, but not just incrementally.

So if you do decide to grow; what's the best way to achieve that? It obviously depends a lot on who you are as a person and your individual circumstances, but here's a simple way to think about it.

Advantages of Growing by Buying

Here are a few of the typical advantages of buying growth with an acquisition:

- It's much faster. You're adding bulk in chunks rather than one person at a time.
- You're adding revenue while adding people. Individual hires don't typically bring revenue with them.
- You're getting a functioning culture where the people already know each other and have adapted to ways of working together. That doesn't mean it'll match your existing culture precisely, but it will be a known quantity with fewer surprises.
- You'll have a fresh set of client options to whom you can sell your existing services, especially if the firm you're buying isn't an exact duplicate of your own.
- There will be more rungs on the career ladder for the team—because you are a bigger firm, now—and this is one of the reasons they stay around.
- You're borrowing an entire batch of new logos for your wall and client success stories that go with them, making sales easier.
- You're going to end up with a big PR story. The marketplace is impressed with firms on the hunt, and it screams "this firm is successful." This is why you don't hear acquihires described as anything but acquisitions.

That's a pretty powerful combination of advantages, but it's not always the way to go. Slow and steady might make more sense, and it's the default path outside of some other, pressing concern.

If you're in the market to purchase a firm, instead, you can flip everything you've learned in this primer around and be a smarter buyer.

Advantages of Growing by Building

What if you decide to do this more slowly and in your own image, so to speak? Here are the reasons why someone might choose that route:

- You're making a careful choice with each person. You aren't inheriting a big group of people who were assembled for possibly different reasons. Yes, this is slower, but you're looking at each building block as you construct another building on the property rather than having one preassembled and then dropped off with a crane and a big trailer. You aren't required to keep or even take each person in the transaction, but you typically will except for the clear overlaps (accounting, HR, support, etc.).
- There's less financial risk. An individual hire could obviously go wrong, but that's less traumatic than a

purchase going bad. Especially if the cash at closing is funded with borrowed money.

- You'll have lots of hiring to do, but there's less risk of the distraction that comes from working with M&A advisors, tax accountants, and legal minds.
- You can change paths along the way as you learn what works and what doesn't.

Finally

Here's a good order to work through when you start looking at your options:

- Do you want to grow? Stop right there if you're comfortable where you are.
- If you do want to grow, do you just need to add capacity? If so, either build with the right people or maybe acquihire a firm to save money and lower the risk.
- If you need to add a specific capability (to round out your service offering design), maybe think about buying a small team that can hit the ground running. But they'll either need to bring with them a set of decent clients to fund the purchase, or you'll need to find work to throw their way quickly. Successful acquisitions don't usually happen that fast, though, unless you're already in informal discussions with someone.
- If you want to grow quickly and you're drawn to the marketplace splash that an acquisition will spark, even if it's just adding more of the same, think about a real acquisition. As long as you're working with a professional so the process doesn't overly distract you personally (which we discussed in Chapter 08

"Consider Opportunities & Manage Distractions"), you'll learn a lot and possibly create even more distance between your firm and the competition.

Everything you've read here can help you in the acquiring process, too, and that might very well be in your near future, especially if it contributes to an eventual exit for yourself.

Now back to what you'll be doing personally after this transaction eventually closes.

25

YOUR ROLE AFTER THE TRANSACTION

I'm often amused by the people who write books about "finding your purpose," and especially by *when* they write them. These are frequently written by recent sellers of firms who now feel adrift. There was obviously a significant overlap between their business and their sense of self, and now that first part is gone. They didn't just sell their firm—they sold their identity, so to speak, and need to find it again. And now they have a bunch of time and money on their hands, and it's kind of a luxury to write about "finding your purpose" when you find yourself in that place.

I understand the allure of these books; selling your paddle to a passing boat because you need the money is going to bite you when a storm comes up or you want to go somewhere. But it's pretty easy to sit around and dream about your purpose in life when you now have millions of dollars in the bank, no forced responsibilities, and thus plenty of time on your hands.

The truth is that finding your purpose is a luxury that normal people just working to put food on the table don't have, and I wish we'd dismantle this idea that we should only do what we love and will surely find success in doing so. It's bullshit.

And yet, since you've likely not sold a firm before, you won't know what to expect and how to create that sense of fulfillment.

When you sell your firm—unless it's for some emergency that crops up, like a big health scare—you are usually ready to move on. And so here's how that typically looks:

- You'll wish you'd done it sooner.
- You don't miss much about that life (except the spotlight and, maybe, the impact).
- The earnout can't end soon enough.
- You're excited about what's next.
- You're driving your life partner crazy.

Your role—and even your identity—might change after the transaction closes and you find yourself in an earnout, and then it will change again after you move on to your next challenge.

One of the *common* reasons to move on from your current firm is that you're now just empty and can't find the engagement to keep going. You like building things more than maintaining things. Even though you whined about it, you loved the thrill of fast-paced "figure it out" stuff in the early days, patching holes in the ship, making crazy promises, coming together as a team of people who were more hard-working than they were skilled.

But one of the *best* reasons to move on from your current firm is that you're just "full up," as they say. You've accomplished a lot, against significant odds. You've built a firm that didn't miss any payrolls. You employed some fantastic people. You have adoring clients, generally, and a few that kinda hate you (because you did the right thing). You've given, given, given, and you're satisfied. You've run a good race.

An official marathon is defined as 26 miles and 385 yards, but nobody gets to tell you how long *your* race is. Once you start to see the finish line everywhere, around every corner, maybe it's time to admit that your imagination is telling you something—and to pay attention.

Your Next Two Jobs

So what are you going to do after the deal closes and you're in the middle of the earnout? (Or "serving your sentence," as some people have called it.)

The answer to that will depend in part on whether you're the sole owner making the transition or whether or not there are other partners coming with you. A partner overseeing some technical or practice area will likely do the same thing. One who is in finance or HR or operations might continue in that role for your small firm, as part of the larger one, but you can expect their role to eventually be subsumed into how the HQ does it.

If you are the sole owner of a firm being purchased, here's what you can almost always expect to keep doing: selling. There might be a little bit of marketing mixed into the sales part (say you've always wanted to write that book or you love speaking on stage regularly), but selling will be job No. 1.

Not only will the buyer want you to sell, it will also be in your best interest to hit those earnout targets. Your role could consist of helping them upsell your current clients on the acquirer's services or even selling what you do to their clients. You might also be folded into a team, where you help close the bigger deals involving all of your new combined services. In fact, selling will probably be your primary responsibility, which is also why you need to understand the incentives in the earnout structure. In Chapter 20 "Crafting a Reasonable Earnout," we talked about the inevitable tension that will arise when they ask you to take on a task that doesn't help you achieve your own earnout numbers.

Your second job—though this not is always the case—could be to help them identify and close subsequent acquisition opportunities. This will only be true if the purchase of your firm is one of many, but it's a common request. And this is really fun to do. You will have a certain amount of credibility because you yourself have gone through that process, and the new acquisition target is far more likely to trust your perspective than the buyer's.

Actually, selling is fun, too. If you've built a firm that's sellable, there's a high likelihood that you're good at selling and enjoy doing it.

Those are the two core things that'll be expected of you, though there might be others.

Starting something should be glorious. Ending something at the right time should be just as glorious because it gives you a new and exciting challenge, built right smack on top of all the skills you've already mastered.

26

LOOPHOLES TO MAXIMIZE AN EARNOUT

I want to say something important before we get started in this chapter: You should always default to negotiating in good faith, which will invariably lead straight to an earnout that's also navigated in good faith.

If, during the negotiations, you start getting nervous about the buyer, that's the time to dive deeper into that gut instinct, to either resolve it or maybe walk away. That scenario might look like:

- Untruths about something. The buyer tells you one thing and you learn that there's an important backstory that shines a different light on what you were led to believe.
- There's an unfriendly firmness in resolving some of the nuances in an agreement. A purchase agreement might run 40 or even 80 pages, and they are exhausting to read, much less to write. It's counterproductive to try to anticipate every single element that might surface after the transaction closes. So there absolutely will be scenarios where

> the other party will have an opportunity to follow the letter or the spirit of the agreement, and what they do in those moments will be revealing.

When the two parties keep dragging the agreement out and pointing to specific language in a dispute, you have entered a new zone. Of course, you could be the bad actor in this situation, in which case I'm just going to say stop it and be a fair human. But if the other party is squeezing you unreasonably, and bad blood is starting to rule the day, and you've decided in your head and your heart that you don't want to work here after the earnout ends, and if the earnout is starting to feel more like imprisonment than an opportunity to do great things together, you might very well need to protect yourself.

The reason I'm writing this at the outset of the chapter is because it must be seen as a Plan B. It should not be the default behavior on your part. But two can play this game, and if someone pulls out a weapon in what was earlier described as a fist fight, well, someone changed the rules and it wasn't you.

If your relationship with the buyer (your new boss) becomes adversarial after the purchase, you may need to protect yourself.

So please read this as a defense if you need it, and not how you should normally act. The other way you could read this, if the tables are reversed and you're the buyer, is to tighten up your agreements to prevent some of the loopholes I'm going to describe below.

You'll already know the normal ways to maximize your earnout, and that's not what we're talking about in this chapter. This chapter suggests some ways in which you can give yourself an unfair advantage if the buyer is going to get all technical and "by the book" on you and try to minimize what you can earn. Press this too far and you'll end up in a legal dispute, which no one wants and hardly anyone wins, but sometimes all you need to do is to give yourself some better leverage as you look to clarify your standing within an earnout. In other words, you might simply suggest that you'll have to resort to one or more of these tactics, and that might be enough to move the discussion closer to a resolution.

Arbitrage Your Labor

Chances are good that your earnout is tied to profitability. The projections you've made to anticipate what you might receive in an earnout are based on using the same labor force that you brought into the transaction. This is the same labor force that you have worked hard to protect by assessing the buyer's culture thoroughly and arranging reporting relationships to minimize disruption and so on. But if the deal has now turned a bit adversarial, some of your people may not want to stay, and it might be appropriate to near- or far-shore your labor and arbitrage the difference in cost (selling to clients at the same price while costing you less to staff the function). It's unlikely that this will ever have been addressed in a purchase agreement, and so it'll be there for the taking.

Accept Client Concentration

A client concentration challenge is defined as having one related source of work represent 15% or more of your total billing. That target varies by subindustry within the professional services space. Normally, you'd want to avoid this problem for several reasons:

- Your firm will be at risk if the client leaves.
- You'll slowly be drawn away from an expertise role into more of an order-taking role as you functionally become their in-house department.

The risk identified in that first point might still be there during the earnout. But in an adversarial setting, you'll be more interested in what happens now and less interested in what happens to the acquiring firm after your earnout is done.

It's much easier to sell while walking the proverbial halls of an existing client than it is to land a new one. Satisfied internal contacts can introduce you to their colleagues, you're present in their planning meetings and might get first crack at leading a new initiative, and there's just a massive "go with the flow" kind of momentum you can take advantage of.

And if you aren't too concerned with what happens after the earnout, and if all your business-building efforts within that one entity will help you in the short term, why not?

Defer or Skip Large Expenses

Again, this is not how you'd want to run things under normal circumstances, but you've now been handed an incentive to maximize the short term. Since your earnout will likely be tied to some profit or EBITDA number, maybe don't transition to that far more expensive SaaS platform that you've been wanting to use, cut that conference sponsorship that is about building long-term relationships with the right people, spend less on your marketing plan when you no longer care about the long tail, don't spend as much money on training and development, cut the entertainment back, and convert client travel to online meetings.

These are not the responsible steps to take when you're in it for the long haul, but they are exactly what you'd do in a downturn—in this case the downturn is in the relationship and not the economy.

Lease vs. Expense

Section 179 changes in recent years have allowed businesses like yours to spend a lot more on equipment purchases and expense them in full when they occur, rather than spreading the expense out over time. The tax incentive underlying those changes was meant to promote purchases that are good for the economy and good for your firm's performance while giving you a legitimate way to reduce your taxable profit.

But you can also look at that same taxable profit as a big number in your earnout calculations, and taxation isn't quite so top of mind like it was when you were running your own firm. So instead of buying things outright and capturing all that taxation advantage, reducing your profit in the process, consider renting or leasing what you need, instead. You have to be careful with that because there are operating leases and capital leases and the transaction needs to be done carefully, but this is another way to boost your earnout calculations while deferring some of the expenses that you would have swallowed whole and move them forward to hit the books after your earnout is complete.

Quicker Staffing Adjustments

Here I'll mention again we're past the culture-building phase and we're in a "grab what you can" stage. The staffing continuity isn't as important because your team feels like you do about the long-term prospects of working at the buyer's firm past your earnout.

This means that you might make a quicker staffing adjustment rather than hang on and ride out a downturn. Or maybe you use more of a Hollywood staffing model, where you assemble freelancers for each big project and they move on when the project is done.

Maybe you don't jump at hiring that once-in-a-lifetime-opportunity star that you don't need quite yet, where in the past you would have added them to the team and then found clients who needed that capability.

Narrowly Targeted Marketing Activity

Normally you'd want all the marketing activities to be coordinated from the top and to build the firm's brand as a whole. But if your incentives change and now you're forced to be a bit more self-protective, you might tailor some outbound initiatives more narrowly.

You might participate less in cross-selling in ways that serve the firm's future outside your own earnout considerations and instead gather opportunity for your area of control. It can't be unbranded from the whole, but there's no reason you can't go after narrow engagements where a new client doesn't use all the service offerings under the company umbrella, focusing instead on just using yours. This would entail a highly concentrated sales effort where you aren't spending any extra time or money on spillover effects for the other parts of the company that are outside your earnout calculations.

Shift Engagement Timing

Here I want to emphasize again that you're staying within the letter of the law in your earnout agreement so that you can live with yourself and defend your actions—but there's no reason that you can't be more self-interested in when an engagement is consummated (accrual accounting) or when it is paid (cash accounting).

This would be especially useful if your earnout is structured around cliffs rather than ramps, and missing some target by a small amount results in an inordinate impact on your earnings. You never want to play fast and loose with client deposits and unearned income, but you can phase your engagements to account for how the earnout is calculated, by accelerating—or even deferring—when those hit the spreadsheet that'll be used in the calculations.

Finally

None of these tactics are optimal in a respectful relationship with the buyer of your firm, but you can resort to them if your new bosses decide to play that game. You can even tip your hand about the possibility of using them to improve your negotiating position or extract some concession in how the purchase agreement will be applied, and then carry on as normal.

Now, if you aren't planning for a sale in the immediate future, you might as well spend the time you have in assuring a better outcome when you do, in fact, sell. That's what we'll talk about as we close this book.

27

PREPPING FOR AN EVENTUAL SALE

Say you're reading this long before an exit is on the table, and you're inspired. You're also ready to do whatever you can to maximize that exit when and if it does happen.

I'm going to recap a few key aspects of your business you ought to work on, and you can go back to the earlier chapters to review them in greater depth.

Here's what to do now so you get a better exit later:

- **Clean up your accounting.** Get personal expenses out of the books so you don't have to argue about add backs later. If you've mistakenly purchased a building inside the corporation itself, rather than holding it in a separate corporation and having a lease between the two, fix that. (It should never be in the same corporation.) And if you are not on an accrual basis, quit listening to some old accountant in NYC and fix that. It's unconscionable to be using anything but accrual and your potential buyer is going to (rightly) make assumptions about your financial sophistication if you're on a cash basis. (Being on a cash basis for taxes is fine, but not for running your firm on a daily basis.) You might even move your vehicle off the corporate books and lease/own it personally, giving yourself a vehicle allowance instead. Run legitimate personal expenses through the company and pull the rest. That "corporate meeting" was really just a vacation. Finally, if there are expensive assets inside the corporation that the buyer will not want to purchase (like artwork), pull them out now.

- **Package your IP correctly.** If there are separate expenses and/or income from your IP, and if you're worried that the buyer might not share your perspective on its value, you might want to put it in a separate corporation and license it to the working entity. This would also allow you to give the buyer a nonexclusive and maybe lifetime right to use that IP, while not limiting your own ability to maximize its value later. If nothing else, doing this will make it harder for you to keep fooling yourself about how valuable it really is.
- **Keep your pay high.** The primary reason is to keep you from getting bored with the business and resenting what it takes from you without a fair return for your personal investment of time and mental energy. But this will also signal the level of compensation you'll need from the buyer in the form of an employment agreement. At minimum, make sure your pay isn't so low that you're effectively subsidizing the EBITDA, because that will likely be recalculated and the advantage will go to the buyer.
- **Craft your client engagements in a manner that seems more predictable**, but only to whatever

extent that's in the client's best interest. This might mean recurring monthly or annual engagements, auto-renewing contracts with a set notification period, and so on. Turn the tables on your firm and imagine that you're doing a "quality of earnings" audit, and then be ready to answer questions like your cost of client acquisition, client churn percentages, lifetime value of the typical client, and the average client growth over the lifetime of that relationship.

- **Build a scalable marketing plan** that doesn't depend as much on you, personally. You'll still be central to closing opportunities, and you should expect to be closely engaged in selling as an executive function, but the marketing should be separate, efficient, predictable, and easily describable to the buyer. Organic, word of mouth, client contacts changing companies, and referrals are flattering, but they are not impressive as a system.
- **Craft an increasingly tighter positioning** for your company. Yes, in doing so you'll be less attractive to the hordes of business opportunities that others might pursue, but you'll become more intensely attractive to the right buyers, you'll be able to craft a far more addressable marketing plan, and your staffing will be unique in order to deliver on those promises. Know what you do for whom, and be able to describe this in a way that's different from your peers. An earlier book, *The Business of Expertise: How Entrepreneurial Experts Convert Insight to Impact and Wealth*, covers this extensively, especially in the first few chapters.

- **Pay attention to any client concentration risks** that might sneak up on you. It's not like you'll suddenly begin turning down that work, but you might have a stronger marketing plan than normal, as well as a thicker cash cushion. You might even acquihire a firm to smooth out the curve if a large client leaves you suddenly.
- **Curate a leadership team** of four to six strong performers who are each in charge of a functional portion of your firm. These are the people who have a longer engagement trajectory than you do and who will carry the firm through an earnout after the transaction boundary. And then test their capabilities by taking a sabbatical to re-energize your approach to the firm and keep it healthy.
- **Build a company that consistently delivers double-digit EBITDA** year after year, seldom dipping below 20%, and only then with a reasonable explanation for why it happened. Your EBITDA is the biggest lever you'll exercise in negotiations.

As I noted at the outset of this book, running your firm that way might mean you never want to sell it in the first place. But if you do decide to sell it, you'll certainly maximize that once-in-a-lifetime opportunity that most people can just dream of. And if you don't, you'll appreciate the entrepreneurial adventure because you've turned your gaze onto building an amazing firm that does great work, rather than actually doing that great work yourself.

I wish you the very best in your journey, and if we can help you realize this dream at Punctuation.com, please reach out and introduce yourself.

GLOSSARY OF KEY M/A TERMS

This glossary doesn't define every term in the M&A space, but rather just the ones that you should understand when you hear them so that you aren't embarrassed and/or someone takes advantage of you. Some of these are quite advanced, but most of them are very basic. These are included to make sure you capture any nuance before someone corrects you.

Acquihire. Used to describe the purchase of a firm, but the actual transaction costs the buyer less than a traditional acquisition, and it delivers more than an absorption to the seller. It combines two terms, acquisition and hire. The purchased firm is usually "defective" in the sense that there has been some intractable challenge (usually new business) and the entrepreneur wishes to exist, and then thrive, in a larger, more protective environment. To the seller, an acquihire is better than all the staff members merely being hired by the buyer, but not as lucrative as a traditional sale to the buyer.

Asset Sale. The purchase of whatever another legal entity owns, but without actually purchasing the corporation that owns those things. An asset sale, for consideration, transfers things like furniture, fixtures, hardware, software, client lists, IP, and so on, but moves them from the seller's corporation to the buyer's corporation without incurring any risk that might accompany the actual shares of the selling firm, including tax liabilities or legal judgments.

Balance Sheet. The consolidated statement of the assets and liabilities of a corporate entity. Under assets, you might find cash, accounts receivable, fixed assets, etc. Under liabilities, you might find accounts payable, credit cards, installment loans, leases, unearned client deposits, etc.

By-Laws (or partnership agreement). The written document that governs how an organization functions and decisions are made by the entity. This document is agreed to, in writing, by all owners of that entity, and is then bound by the specifics in that document. It will ideally address how voting is conducted, how members are replaced, how shares are sold and at what price and terms, etc.

Cap Table. A spreadsheet, usually, that shows what percentage of the company is owned by which entities, as well as the nature of their shares (controlling, voting, non-voting, etc.).

Capital Call. Refers to the infusion of cash, from the shareholders, personally, to the corporation. This is usually booked on the financial statements as Paid In Capital to distinguish the reversal of the capital call as repayment of a loan, recognized as such or not, rather than a distribution. A capital call is usually structured to match the ownership percentages of the shareholders. So if there are two equal partners, each would contribute an equal amount.

Cash at Closing. The portion of the purchase price that is paid at the transaction boundary, when the buyer acquires part or all of a seller's interest in the firm. Anything not included in "cash at closing" is usually subject to the seller hitting certain performance targets in the earnout. This is proposed in the LOI (letter of intent), and is confirmed in the purchase agreement, which is signed at that transaction event and after the due diligence period has concluded and when the purchase is consummated.

Conflict Strategy. The assurances you make to clients who might compete in the marketplace, but who rely on you for advice. A conflict strategy is sometimes required to allay any fears that one client might have if your positioning, by definition, attracts more than one firm competing in the same space. This written strategy lays out how you will serve their best interests strategically without compromising any of the competitive advantages they might hold because you are also working for one or more of their competitors.

Corporation Type. Corporations are merely legal entities that are formed for a specific purpose. They are formed by the owner(s), and then they assemble a team of people to carry out that purpose. Corporations are not all the same, though, and carry unique legal protections and taxation features. The buyer must determine if it is in their best interest to purchase that legal entity in a stock sale or just purchase some of what the corporation owns in an asset sale. A legal entity chooses its format when it is created, though that can often be changed later, and in the USA, a corporation is a state-based entity.

Cross-Selling. Sell a different service or product to an existing customer. After a transaction, the buyer might want to sell what they offer to your clients, or they might want you, the seller, to line up customers from their existing base to purchase what you are selling. Cross-selling takes advantage of the existing relationships of both parties.

Dissolution. The opposite of a founding. A dissolution is a specific action to close a firm and wind down its operations. An "orderly dissolution" is one undertaken of your own choosing, and not forced on it via, for example, an involuntary bankruptcy. An orderly dissolution is undertaken, usually, because no acquisition opportunity surfaced, or because the would-be seller is not open to any type of earnout and no buyer has surfaced who will pay 100% of the transaction price at closing. So instead, the owner pays its obligations from its assets and retains the remainder.

Drag Along Clause. This is a mechanism whereby minority shareholders are obligated to follow the choices of majority shareholders. They can disagree and dialogue, but in the end they have no legal standing to kill a decision made by the majority shareholders. Say, for example, that there's a 5% shareholder and the remaining 95% of the firm is owned by one entity, and that majority shareholder decides to sell the firm to an outsider. The 5% shareholder cannot kill the deal, though in practice they might have some non-legal leverage because the buyer might not want an unwilling participant, who is typically relevant to the selling firm's operations or they would not have been granted 5% of the shares in the first place.

Due Diligence. The examination that a buyer conducts, after the LOI (letter of intent) is signed, but before the sale is consummated when a purchase agreement is executed. This allows the buyer to verify any assumptions they have made, discover important elements of the firm they are intending to purchase, and possibly revise the offer based on what they find.

It is usually conducted by the buyer's agents, including legal, tax, and advisory experts. There is no set period for due diligence, but often an LOI will suggest a closing date, before which the due diligence would be completed. Typically due diligence will last from one to four months, depending on the complexity of the transaction, and the seller will be required to sign a no-shop clause.

Earnout. Any of the purchase price that is a) not paid in cash at closing and b) subject to certain performance targets. The requirement could be as simple as maintaining employment in good standing, or as complex as hitting very specific profit targets over multiple years. The targets might be something besides profit, too, like retaining a client, developing a service, etc.

EBITDA. This abbreviation refers to "earnings before interest, taxes, depreciation, and amortization." These four things, typically included in expenses before net profit is calculated, are actually pulled from expenses, thereby raising the profit number. The profit that doesn't account for these four expenses is referred to as EBITDA.

Employment Agreement. The legal document that specifies the employment arrangements undertaken between the new firm, after an acquisition, and a key executive of the firm that is being purchased. This establishes a pay level, benefits, the length of the employment, the duties expected of the person, and how employment can come to an end, initiated by either party. In an acquisition, an employment agreement helps the seller understand how much influence they will have on hitting the targets that will be earned during the earnout period.

ESOP. A specific tax-advantaged process in which a company transfers its shares to an employee pool, also specifying how the company will run its affairs and deal with later transactions as ownership interests shift. A seller might opt for an ESOP, selling all or part of their shares, the purchase of which is often funded by a third entity, using the sold shares as collateral. A later, less complicated variant of this process, is accomplished through the establishment of an ownership cooperative.

Goodwill. Represents the portion of a purchase price beyond the actual value of the fixed, tangible assets owned by a corporation. This term refers to the intangible value that both a buyer and seller agree on in a transaction.

Gross Profit. While this is defined in many different ways, it is usually defined in the professional services space as all the revenue that remains after the direct costs of goods sold are deducted. These COGS are pass-through items that can be tied directly to a specific client, in whose absence such a purchase would not have been made. This excludes any overhead costs that are utilized in servicing all clients, generally. So gross profit would account for the cost of a product or service purchased specifically to be resold to a client, excluding internal labor. In some cases, gross profit is also referred to as fee billings. Gross profit is distinguished from net profit in that net profit recognizes all expenses, and not just the expenses of products or services resold to specific clients.

Income Statement. A financial report that summarizes the profit or loss incurred over a specific period of time. It recognizes the income and expense, as well as the gains and losses, in that specific period. Managers use an income statement to make important decisions about the profit contribution of an enterprise to the shareholders of that enterprise. An income statement can be built on an accrual or cash basis, but accrual is always the preferred method because it properly recognizes more elements, and because it tracks performance closer to the events that have occurred.

Intellectual Property. Also referred to as IP, this refers to the intangible creations that a company holds, developed by its members or purchased from an outside party, usually utilized to provide an advantage over its competitors.

Investor. An outside entity who infuses cash in exchange for a percentage ownership, expecting a return on that investment, either from profit distributions and/or later resale at a higher price per share.

LOI. Letter of intent, written by a potential buyer and offered to a seller, that lays out the specific intent to purchase some portion of a buyer's interest, spelling out that purchase in specific terms, subject to any discoveries they make during a due diligence period. An LOI is typically non-binding, though it might require the seller to enter into an exclusive "no-shop" period. Larger transactions might provide for a break-up fee should the buyer not move forward with the purchase, offsetting the time and money that a seller incurred during the process.

Merger. The combination of two or more legal entities who will redistribute ownership interests and begin to operate as a single entity. A merger is simply a transaction where there is no clear buyer or seller. Instead of a one-way purchase price, from buyer to seller, there is an exchange of assets for specified equity.

Multiple. The amount by which the EBITDA of a purchase target is multiplied to arrive at a purchase price. If the EBITDA of a target company is $1M and the multiple is 4x, the purchase price is expressed as $4M. There are standard multiple ranges for each vertical industry, and then terms are applied to note how and when and on what basis the purchase price is actually paid.

Net Profit. See gross profit above.

Non-Disclosure Agreement. An executed legal agreement whereby one party agrees to keep the information they will learn confidential and out of the public eye. This is usually limited to information that's not already known to the public, and a mutual NDA binds both parties and not just one party. These are executed when one party needs to access confidential information in order to determine how to proceed, and the party with that information wants to limit how it is circulated. Executed NDAs usually allow you to consult with your advisors.

No-Shop Clause. A period of time when you will not actively look for another buyer, and when you will tell the potential buyer if another buyer approaches you with the intent to purchase your firm, setting up a competitive situation where the potential buyer who asks you to sign the NDA does not want to invest time or money without some advantage in the process. You would not want to sign such an agreement if you want to search for other buyers in an attempt to surface other bids.

Orderly Dissolution. See dissolution, above.

Profit/Loss (or P/L). See income statement, above.

Partner. Someone who actually owns a percentage of the firm, however large or small. While individuals are sometimes called "partner" without any equity attached, here we are referring to someone with actual equity. This excludes anyone who is merely a participant in profit-sharing, options, profit-interests, etc.

Partnership agreement (or by-laws). See by-laws, above.

Private Equity (PE). This is the capital that is raised from others (individuals and entities) by PE firms, then used to invest in private companies (not those listed on publicly traded exchanges). PE investments are made with an investment horizon in mind, at which time they expect to resell those holdings for a profit, which is then redistributed back to the original investors in a fund.

Purchase Agreement. The legal document that represents all the final details of a proposed transaction, signed at closing by the buyer and seller, after due diligence is complete, which is conducted after a proposed buyer delivers an LOI to a proposed seller. This document is prepared by the buyer's attorney, approved in advance by the seller's attorney, and is often separate from the employment agreement that is also signed concurrently.

Retained Equity. The portion a seller retains rather than selling that to the buyer. So a buyer might purchase 51% of a firm, leaving the seller with 49% retained equity. The later sale price and terms of that retained equity are usually addressed in a purchase agreement. This is separate from rollover equity (see below).

Rollover Equity. The portion of a purchase price not actually paid for at closing, but essentially reinvested into the larger buyer's entity. The seller might be given what is sometimes referred to as a "second bite of the apple." Say that the purchase agreement specifies that 10% of a seller's position is "rolled over" into the equity of the seller. That 10% would represent a much smaller percentage of the buyer's firm or other ownership interest, and the seller is paid for that rollover equity later, in a subsequent transaction, that might or might not happen. It allows the buyer to align their interests with the seller because both parties are aiming for a favorable later sale of that entity, of which the seller now owns a small portion. This is separate from retained equity (see above).

Roll-Up. The process whereby a buyer initiates multiple purchases of similar or related firms, for the purpose of selling the combined entity later at a higher price than the firms would have sold for individually. The lead buyer purchases each firm, over time, and may ask the sellers of each firm to accept rollover equity in exchange for some portion of their shares. In some cases, the book value of the purchased firms is used to purchase subsequent firms, and in other cases the transactions are funded with debt.

SPAC. Special purpose acquisition vehicle, or essentially a shell corporation that begins trading on a stock exchange, and only then uses its assets to purchase a private company. This allows a private company's shares to essentially be traded on a public exchange without going through the actual process of being listed on such an exchange. Some roll-ups (see above) attempt to exit their investment in this manner, though a SPAC cannot legally be formed with the intent of acquiring a specific company.

Stock Sale. See asset sale, above.

Strategic Purchase. Any purchase that commands a price higher than a strict mathematical valuation. In other words, any purchase motivated by something other than buying a stream of profit.

Terms. The arrangements upon which a purchase price is paid. Some of the purchase price might be paid in cash at closing and some may be subject to hitting certain performance targets in an earnout. In still other cases, there might be a seller note, guaranteed or not, that specifies certain installment arrangements. See "valuation," below.

Valuation. The process of determining what an entity is worth. This is more commonly relevant to a private company that's not traded on a public exchange, since a publicly traded company's value is essentially all its outstanding stock times the share price. Valuations are conducted by experts in a particular vertical category, and can take many things into account, including book value, a multiple of EBITDA, free cashflow, discretionary earnings, normalized shareholder compensation, etc. A specific valuation methodology is usually favored based on how a company's operation and growth is funded. See "terms," above.

DISCLAIMER

Now I have to say exactly what you'd expect me to say. Read this book really carefully as a helpful tome, but then don't rely on it exclusively. The information here is general in nature and shouldn't be considered legal or tax advice. You really should consult with an attorney or tax professional regarding your individual situation, and of course you need to find an advisor who knows what they are doing.

ACKNOWLEDGMENTS

Finally, I want to publicly, again, acknowledge how influential Blair Enns has been in my work. His thinking worms its way into mine, constantly, and our decades of collaboration on content, events, and the 2Bobs podcast has enriched me, as has our friendship over all that time.

Special thanks go to Bryn Mooth for her ability to take the outcome of what happens when my brain triggers my fingers in wild spasms and somehow makes it into something that reaches humans, always accepting of my unique grammar and punctuation cadence; Emily Mills who reads *my* ideas and helps *you* see them with the perfect illustration; Spencer Fuller at Faceout Studios for the cover design; Pollock Printing in Nashville; and Marcus DePaula for his meticulous audio editing skills.

Finally, to you the reader, I offer my deepest thanks. Granting me your money—but mainly your time and attention—is the best return a writer could ever want. I am so grateful for your trust, and we will keep working hard to earn it in all we do at Punctuation. If we can help you with a transaction of any type, please reach out. But regardless of who you work with, I hope you enter that new adventure more prepared and ready for what you'll be facing, only to emerge on the other side rich and happy.